Praise for *Faith in the Spotlight*

"This book is great! Real, practical, sound insight from someone who is salt and light in their workplace. Ever since I met Megan I have been impressed by her bold faith."

—Luis Palau, international evangelist and author

"As a Christian woman working in a secular industry, I quite literally take my 'seat at the table,' serving as cohost of *The View*. *Faith in the Spotlight* provides an honest take on what it's like to be a career woman of faith in the twenty-first century, sharing real-life scenarios combined with God-honoring solutions that I, too, have faced throughout my career. This is a refreshing read that highlights the importance of living on a mission for Christ in the workplace and using our influence wherever God calls us."

—Candace Cameron Bure, actress, author, and cohost of *The View*

"This book is an excellent and thoughtful read for anyone who desires to work in the entertainment industry and beyond. Megan offers superb wisdom and advice."

—Alecia Davis, national correspondent for *Extra*

"How do we engage the culture? Not retreat, because of what we fear. Not give in, because of what we can't live without. But be our created selves, where the Creator has placed us. Megan has honestly wrestled with that question from day one. And the fruit is apparent. In her life. In this book. This is a must-read!"

—Stan D. Gaede, president, Christian College Consortium

"Megan's book inspires young women to think big and live out their purpose while achieving their dreams! A must-read for this next generation."

—Dana and Ryan Malouff, lead pastors of Expression Church, Austin, Texas

FAITH *in the* SPOTLIGHT

Thriving in Your Career While Staying True to Your Beliefs

MEGAN ALEXANDER

HOWARD BOOKS

An Imprint of Simon & Schuster, Inc.

New York   Nashville   London   Toronto   Sydney   New Delhi

Howard Books
An Imprint of Simon & Schuster, Inc.
1230 Avenue of the Americas
New York, NY 10020

Author is represented by Ambassador Literary, Nashville, TN.

Insert photographs are courtesy of the author unless otherwise noted.

First Howard Books hardcover edition October 2016

HOWARD and colophon are trademarks of Simon & Schuster, Inc.

For information about special discounts for bulk purchases, please contact Simon & Schuster Special Sales at 1-866-506-1949 or business@simonandschuster.com.

The Simon & Schuster Speakers Bureau can bring authors to your live event. For more information or to book an event, contact the Simon & Schuster Speakers Bureau at 1-866-248-3049 or visit our website at www.simonspeakers.com.

Interior design by Davina Mock-Maniscalco

Manufactured in the United States of America

10 9 8 7 6 5 4 3 2 1

Library of Congress Cataloging-in-Publication Data

Names: Alexander, Megan, author.
Title: Faith in the spotlight : thriving in your career while staying true to your beliefs / Megan Alexander.
Description: New York : Howard Books, [2016]
Identifiers: LCCN 2016019847| ISBN 9781501143052 (hardcover : alk. paper)
ISBN 9781501143076 (ebook)
Subjects: LCSH: Christianity and culture.
Classification: LCC BR115.C8 A4334 2016 | DDC 248.4—dc23 LC record available at https://lccn.loc.gov/2016019847

ISBN 978-1-5011-4305-2
ISBN 978-1-5011-4307-6 (ebook)

Dedicated to my boys: Chace, Catcher, and Brian.
The best team I could ever hope for!

Contents

Preface

*O*NE OF MY FAVORITE THINGS to do is to walk the aisles of a bookstore. Yes, we are seeing fewer bookstores these days—but I still like to be inside a brick-and-mortar store, holding a book in my hands, reading the back cover, and checking out nearby titles.

I often head to the Self-Help aisle, the Leadership and Business section, and the Faith and Religion shelves. There I find stories of the people who have gone before me and pages that offer an opportunity to learn from, laugh with, and share in triumphs and struggles. I go there seeking inspiration for both my professional and personal lives.

But I've noticed an all-too familiar narrative: secular bookstores are bursting with titles for the career-minded woman. I have really enjoyed many of them, such as *The Trump Card* by Ivanka Trump, *Knowing Your Value* by Mika Brzezinski, and *Fierce Optimism* by Leeza Gibbons. But when I look for books about Christian women in leadership roles or books for the career-minded woman of faith, I can't find any!

There are plenty of books for Christians, and I have relied on those; *Produced by Faith* by DeVon Franklin and *Intentional Living* by John Maxwell are good ones that I have found very useful. Their pages certainly have takeaways for both women and men. But a book with real-life examples and practical advice written specifically for an ambitious Christian businesswoman who is working in a competitive industry, desiring to climb the corporate ladder, and wanting to excel in her career while maintaining her family and faith? I can't seem to find one.

I definitely could have used a book for professional Christian women several times in my career when I needed to make some tough business decisions and seek advice from someone I knew was grounded in their faith. I still need this advice!

Needed: Role Models

I recently received an email that crystallized for me the reality of this need. A pastor in Seattle emailed about his three daughters who have big dreams and ambitious career goals. They are also Christians. He explained that he wants to encourage and inspire them to achieve great things in this world as female leaders, but he can't find role models for them. Since I was one of the few he could locate, he asked me to speak at their church. I accepted—and told myself, *It's time to do more. I need to write a book.* After all, one of my favorite quotes is by Gandhi and states: "Be the change you want to see in the world." That's what I'm doing—writing about leadership and business for Christian women.

So what qualifies me for this self-appointed task? In a word, experience. Oh, I don't have all the answers. I don't have a *lifetime* of experience. But at thirty-five, I have navigated some pretty interesting situations as a TV reporter, first on a local talk show in San Antonio, Texas, and currently as a correspondent for the national TV show *Inside Edition* and as a special correspondent for CBS's *Thursday Night Football*. I'm an actress, speaker, and producer as well. I have been on set with some of the biggest names in Hollywood, and I have had to handle the stress of my agent pressuring me to accept a role I felt uncomfortable with. I've dealt with tough negotiations over contracts and salary, and I've covered the billion-dollar industry that is the NFL.

And as I've done these things, I have maintained my faith. It hasn't been easy—it still isn't—and I don't know if I've always made the right decisions. But with counsel from the Lord, my family, my friends, and my gut, I've done and continue to do my best. One of my bold decisions that I have no second thoughts about was my choice to save living or sleeping with my husband until we were married, and now we have two babies and are raising a family. And, at times, I have been the primary financial earner for my family. While this has been fulfilling, it has also been very hard work. So I want to pass along what I have learned and am continuing to learn along the way in hopes of saving you some missteps and encouraging you to journey into the business world with confidence and unwavering faith.

Pursuing Your Dreams

Maybe you have big dreams, too. You want to succeed in corporate America, sit at the big boardroom table, or work in Hollywood. So practical advice and stories about what works—from someone who is not too much older than you—would be helpful. This book is for you. And if you are a woman? Even better, because I will tackle some of the important issues you will face in careers of influence: the rat race that is New York City, hustling, body image, getting that first job, taking risks, negotiating contracts, keeping a marriage strong, building a family, and having—and at some point being—a mentor.

Frankly, I am also writing this book because I need you folks with me on this journey! It can be lonely! I need women who are standing strong in their faith as they pursue their dreams and careers, to keep pushing forward when the journey gets tough.

This truly is an exciting time to be a young woman of faith. The opportunities for advancement are endless; the proverbial glass ceiling is and will continue to be shattered. We have women running for president, serving as CEOs of major companies, sitting on boards of directors, and making significant decisions at all levels of business. Women like Roma Downey, Carrie Underwood, and Meagan Good are maintaining their Christian values as they do so. You can do the same. So jump on board with all your dreams, and walk this journey with me.

You can live out your faith in the spotlight and thrive in your career while staying true to your beliefs.

—Megan

*T*he entertainment and media world is more powerful and impactful than ever before. It is literally guiding culture. To have impact, the Bible says, we must be as gentle as doves and wise as serpents (Matthew 10:16). We have done a good job being like doves; now it is time to really get smart. In order to have a positive impact, believers need to master their craft and do it with excellence so they can bring to the table good works that reflect their faith. We were blessed that all our past work on shows like *The Voice*, *The Apprentice*, and *Touched by an Angel* gave us the leverage to produce our passion projects: The Bible series, *The Bible* movie, and *A.D.* Now we are blessed to have produced with MGM Studios and Paramount Pictures a reimagining of the epic tale *Ben-Hur.*

We agree with Megan: we need to be a part of the culture in order to change the culture. We have spoken about this with Megan over the years when she interviewed us about The Bible series and *A.D.* We know God calls us to be salt and light in this world. It is not always easy, but it can be done. Megan's book offers a practical, honest look at one person's experience in the entertainment industry, and her story offers great encouragement for those who want to take that journey, too.

— Roma Downey and Mark Burnett,
founders of Lightworkers Media

One

A Seat at the Table

Why People of Faith Need to Work in Careers of Influence

Be who you were created to be,
and you will set the world on Fire.

—ST. CATHERINE OF SIENA

*N*OT EVERYONE IN THE CHRISTIAN COMMUNITY was supportive of my pursuing a career in media. I remember a family friend saying, "Why on earth would you want to work in that industry? That is Satan's playground!" But I never looked at it that way. I believed God had blessed me with talents to do well as a broadcaster, and I also really enjoyed creating, producing, and working with people. A career in the media seemed like a good career option.

But I did not start my career in TV proclaiming, "I'm a Christian!" or wearing a WWJD bracelet or refusing to do certain stories because of the ungodly subject matter. No. Before I was known for being a woman of faith, I wanted to be known for doing good work. I wanted to become a great reporter, a great interviewer, and a great host. I didn't really talk about my faith that much in the beginning. I never compromised who I was, but I didn't wear my faith on my sleeve at every turn. But along the way I started learning what it meant to make myself available for God to work through me. I've come to believe that we don't have to be a missionary or a pastor to live out the gospel. Wherever God has placed us, we have a platform. You and I can live in a way that honors God—and attracts attention to Him—right where we are. But it took me some time to figure this out.

Who Would I Be on TV?

When I got the job as a morning traffic reporter in San Antonio, Texas, I was prepared to simply do my job, which was report on the morning commute, exchange a few pleasantries with the weatherman and morning anchors, and go about my day. Viewers would hopefully see my warm personality shine through, but there was no room for me to share any personal details beyond some bullet points here and there. But if the anchors asked me what I did over the weekend, I could and might mention that I went to church or attended a Christian concert. A morning newscast moves pretty quickly, and our particular station kept things rather tight, so I only had opportunities to make very brief comments.

Then, not too long into my career as the traffic anchor, I was asked to cohost the local talk show *Great Day SA*. It was an hour of high-energy chitchat about all kinds of topics. We opened the show with an eight-minute segment of ad-libs about our day, what we had done the night before, what segments were coming up on the show, our opinions on things. This was the opposite of the morning news. Suddenly I had to decide exactly who I wanted to be onscreen. Interestingly, the Bible has something to say about deciding who we are: "Make a careful exploration of who you are and the work you have been given, and then sink yourself into that" (Galatians 6:4 MSG).

So who was I? I knew my faith, I knew to live according to God's Word, and I knew to do everything "as working for the Lord" (Colossians 3:23 NIV). But what exactly does that mean in practical, specific, real-life, career-in-the-media terms? I can tell you; it is much easier to just read a teleprompter and follow the script.

When I first started *Great Day SA*, I did not feel comfortable talking about myself and giving my opinions on TV. I was afraid of being singled out and pigeonholed as the "Christian girl," and I worried that could derail my chances for advancement in my overly secular career field. But soon circumstances forced me, in a good way, to decide if I was going to be true to myself and to my faith in my professional life. I also saw those around me trying to figure this out. At one point, one of my coworkers, who had a steady boyfriend, said on air that she was single. After the show, I asked her about it. She confirmed that she had a serious boyfriend, but explained that on air, she wanted to appear very single and available. I was surprised to hear her say this.

I was also dating someone seriously—and he is now my husband. At the time I assumed everyone would be honest about their single/dating/married status. (Munch on that one the next time you see a talk-show host proclaim they are single!) I needed to quickly decide what my answer would be. Would I appear single, too? I had to decide. My boss did actually encourage us to "refrain from talking about our significant others" on air: he liked us to "appear available." Again, I needed to decide what I was going to say—and I hadn't expected to be making decisions like this.

It didn't take me long to decide I wanted to be truthful. God makes it very clear: "The LORD detests lying lips, but he delights in those who tell the truth" (Proverbs 12:22 NLT). After reading this verse, my situation seemed pretty certain. If I had a boyfriend, I needed to be honest. This was being true to myself. My decision was made, and I never looked back. I decided to just be me. Aristotle tells us "Knowing thyself is the beginning of all wisdom." I was beginning to learn what this meant.

Happy Birthday?

During a one-hour *Great Day SA*, we had several five-minute segments. Our producers—primarily our executive producer—selected most of the topics and stories. Occasionally the hosts, or "talent," pitched a story that would make it on the air. But generally we were assigned all the stories we did; we were not really given a choice to say no. It was part of the job to simply accept the assignment, perform our duties for the show, and do so with energy and enthusiasm.

One day our executive producer decided to acknowledge it was Hugh Hefner's birthday. Hugh Hefner's claim to fame is that he is the founder of *Playboy,* a magazine that until recently featured images of nude women. Our executive producer wanted my cohost and me to say happy birthday to Hugh Hefner and talk a bit about him—as we did with all the celebrities whose birthdays we acknowledged. We usually said a few things about what these individuals were known for and what we appreciated about them. Well, my cohost had a picture of herself at the Playboy Mansion in California. She wanted to display it on the screen during the segment so she could talk about how neat it was to see the famed mansion. I immediately felt uncomfortable. But I was a new television talk-show host, so I didn't say anything in our planning meeting. As the "new girl" in the mix, I did not want to ruffle any feathers. I'll be honest; it was tricky—I wanted to please my boss and keep those paychecks coming! Also, having just started working with this group, I wanted to get along with everybody. This is my personality. The idea of being at odds with them was more than a little distressing.

The next day, when we went live, we began the segment by saying happy birthday to Hugh Hefner. My cohost, Kristina, proceeded to talk about the time she went to the Playboy Mansion and how cool it was. When it was my turn, I just could not hold back. "Well, I don't think Hugh is that cool. Some of us don't admire that magazine or what he stands for. I do wish women would value their bodies more highly and refuse to take off their clothes for his magazine. Then maybe he would go out of business!"

Kristina stared at me. She expected these birthday wishes to be a lighthearted segment. She thought I would praise pop culture, as the rest of the world usually does. But I just couldn't. This was the first time on this show that I let my authentic self speak, and I expressed a strong and countercultural opinion. I immediately realized, though, that I wasn't alone in that opinion. You see, we always had a small live audience in the studio. When I said what I did about Hugh Hefner, the whole room burst into applause. More people agreed with me than I had expected!

But all I did was share my opinion. My cohost thought Hugh Hefner was cool and admirable; I did not. Each of us was entitled to our opinion, and hers is definitely more the norm in today's culture. To take the opposite stance felt like a far bigger step than I wish it had. When general opinion leans toward praising Hugh Hefner, it's scary to take and speak the opposite view.

This was my first experience with understanding what it meant to have a "seat at the table" as a person of faith. And I will say that, even though we had different opinions, my cohost was and still is a good friend of mine. She simply had a different opinion. Nothing wrong with that at all.

But herein lies an important point: people complain about the mainstream media, saying they disagree with many of the opinions of talk-show hosts and entertainers on TV—that network television does not fairly represent the Christian faith. But I also understand how hard it is to try to represent faith in God in the TV industry. Suddenly I found myself in a position of influence. I was being asked questions that required authentic answers that reflected my faith, my life, my moral code. I was interacting with people who were making radically different choices in life than I was.

What's interesting is that the combination of my more conservative views and Kristina's more worldly ones ended up making for great and animated conversation on TV. We had a third cohost, Glenn, who was hysterically funny. If things got too intense, he would crack a joke at just the right time. Both of them were and are super-talented TV hosts with great timing and energy. Our ratings were very good for the entire three years we were all together on that show. And viewers frequently commented that they liked the differences in our personalities and opinions. But it did take me a while to realize this and settle into my role.

Equal Time for the Truth

When I started cohosting in 2002, an already established and popular segment was a visit with a local psychic. A frequent guest on the show, he would take calls from viewers who shared their problems or asked questions about loved ones who had passed. The psychic claimed to be able to reveal prophetic answers and even deliver a message from the deceased. This kind of segment is what the industry calls "good TV" in that it resonates with viewers and often results in high ratings, which means lots of people watch.

Callers often cried with gratitude, exclaiming how thankful they were to be able to hear from those beyond the grave. The psychic loved this venue for performing, and his dramatic responses made the segment extremely popular. But I noticed that occasionally people would ask deep questions like "Why do good things happen to bad people?" When the psychic didn't really know how to respond, I thought to myself, *I wish we could do this same segment with a pastor or counselor!* I knew that at the upcoming monthly brainstorming meeting, we would do the usual and discuss story ideas as well as possible guests to interview. I decided that, at the next meeting, I would suggest inviting a pastor onto the show.

I was very familiar with author and pastor Max Lucado. He leads a church in the San Antonio area and is quite well-known in Christian circles. During our brainstorming session, I suggested we invite Max Lucado on and allow viewers to call in and ask him questions about matters of faith, life, family, and more. My suggestion was met with blank stares from my colleagues, who were no doubt thinking: *Who is Max Lucado? What will he talk about? Will viewers really be interested in him?* They were quite skeptical, and the idea was turned down . . . initially.

My boss said to me, "We don't do that. We don't get religious on this show." But I went back to my boss and said, "You know how popular the psychic segment is? I really think people are longing to talk about deeper issues, about spiritual issues. I'm telling you, Max Lucado is very respected and well-known in religious circles and beyond. I do think our viewers will respond to him."

My boss was still not very interested, but one day a last-minute cancellation created an opening on our show. My executive producer asked me if I would contact Max Lucado's people to see if he would come on. Max agreed, he and I had a great interview, and then he invited viewers to call in. They asked all kinds of questions, ranging from, "Why does a loving God allow 9/11 to happen?" to "What do you do if it seems God is not answering your prayers?" Max handled the questions thoughtfully and honestly. He admitted he did not know all the answers and explained that at such moments faith plays its part. Max and the viewers had some great conversations on a variety of life topics.

The next day I learned our ratings had skyrocketed and dozens of viewers had emailed saying how much they enjoyed having Max

Lucado on the show. And that same boss who had said "We don't do religious segments" looked at those amazing ratings and, because he also felt the segment had gone well, said, "Okay, we *do* do those segments!" My boss asked me to arrange for Max Lucado to come on the show again.

It's Not a Conspiracy

I share this story to make this point: I don't believe anyone on that talk show was purposefully scheming to keep Max Lucado or some other religious topic or figure off the show. I think they genuinely did not know who he was, so they did not think he would be of interest to our viewers. How could my colleagues think otherwise? They were not believers and they did not go to church, so talking about religion was not a part of their lives. That's when I began to realize how important it is to have that seat at the table. Simply because I was in the room that day, I was able to suggest a story idea that involved faith and resonated with viewers. You see, I don't believe the media is trying to keep all matters of faith off the air. I do believe that oftentimes, when decisions are being made, not all viewpoints are represented.

I also saw more clearly than ever that my very public job provides an opportunity for a platform. It's also the concept behind the phrase "a seat at the table." I believe I can be most effective in shining for Christ in my career because I have a seat at the table. I am able to be in the room when a decision is made. I am on the scene when a story is being covered. And I am one more voice in the room asking questions. A lot of people talk, write, and even preach about "converting Hollywood" or "bringing morals back to television."

And you know what? Most of the people who have written on this topic have never spent a day working in either industry. They suggest boycotts and campaigns, but I don't think that approach always works.

I think sometimes God uses us most effectively when we are involved in the day-to-day operations—when we get coffee with a colleague, work late at night on a story, or write a script with a coworker. Take a seat at the table where your voice can be heard. Organizational change is most effective coming from the inside, rather than the outside looking in.

Why?

I am very aware that I am not a doctor who has performed life-saving surgeries. Nor am I a foster mom who has cared for dozens of kids or a teacher who has mentored and inspired countless students. But I am involved in an industry that, for good and bad, has a profound impact on our culture and on our young people.

Tim Keller, pastor of Redeemer Presbyterian Church in New York City and a bestselling author, addressed this matter when he answered the question "Why should Christians be in the mix of society and business?" Here is part of Pastor Keller's response:

> Why? As the city goes, so goes the culture. Cultural trends tend to be generated in the city and flow outward to the rest of society. People who live in large urban cultural centers, occupying jobs in the arts, business, academia, publishing, the helping professions, and the media, tend to have a disproportionate impact on how things are done in our culture. Having lived and ministered in New York City for seventeen years, I am continually astonished at how the people living here and in large cities affect what everyone else in the United States sees on the screen, in print, in art, and in business.*

---

* *The Reason for God*, New York: Dutton, 2008.

I so agree! Christians need to be involved—have a seat at the table—in all these different professions. We need to be on the inside. We need to be in the room when decisions are made and impact culture from within.

In the Arena

My purpose in sharing these stories and others throughout the book is to encourage people who want to pursue and thrive in a career. You will have a seat at a table. In fact, you may already have a seat. It doesn't matter how big or small your job or career, we all have areas of influence. For those of you already established in your career, your seat at the table might be in the boardroom, or the break room. Others of you extend influence for the Lord in the classroom as you educate students or colleagues; as a nurse interacting with patients and doctors; or in the courtroom as an attorney advocating for a client.

And for those of you in the process of deciding what career to pursue, follow your dreams and listen for God's direction. He has a plan and a purpose for your life, and wherever you find a seat at the table, it is a big part of His plan. Jeremiah 29:11 reminds us of this truth: "For I know the plans I have for you, declares the LORD. Plans to prosper you and not to harm you, plans to give you hope and a future (NIV)."

So when you take that seat, remember the concept of doing excellent work first. Establish a reputation of excellence and earn the respect of your coworkers and managers. It's not always about winning or achieving. Those are worthy goals, and we should strive for excellence in all that we do. But the point is this: *you are there.* You are in the room. You have earned your place of influence, so carefully consider how you can live out your faith while you are able.

President Theodore Roosevelt spoke about this when he gave a series of lectures in France in 1910. He called his talk "The Christian's role in modern society." He understood and captured this concept well, and his words remain relevant today:

> *It is not the critic who counts, not the man who points out how the strong man stumbles, or where the doer of deeds could have done them better. The credit belongs to the man who's actually in the arena—whose face is marred by dust and blood and sweat, who strives valiantly, who errs, who comes up short again and again. Who, at best, knows in the end the triumph of high achievement, and who, at worst, if he fails, at least fails while daring greatly.*

Takeaway

1. Realize your job, right where you are, can be a platform.

2. Be confident and creative when representing your Faith. I saw an opportunity to contribute with a segment idea, and it ended up being a win-win for all.

3. My opinion is there is no conspiracy against faith in the media. We just need more people of faith to take their seat at the table and do excellent work.

4. Dare greatly and don't get discouraged—just get in the arena and start trying.

*I*n looking back over Meg's life, we vividly recall when her preschool teacher told us she'd had to step out of the classroom for a brief minute or two and when she returned, Meg had the class marching in single file around the room to *The Music Man* theme song "76 Trombones." We have often said Meg came out of the womb ready for the entertainment world. When Meg called in 2004 and said she had a chance to audition for a TV job in San Antonio, we thought, *How appropriate is this? Meant to be!*

In addition to her love of performing, Meg loves the Lord and ways to express this love. There is a saying, when you sing, you are praying twice. Meg sang from her heart in the school choir. At a young age, Meg showed a yearning to memorize Bible verses and then tried to live out the lessons learned. So many times we would read Galatians 5:22–23 and talk about the fruit of the Spirit.

When we watch her on *Inside Edition* or any of her guest appearances, we are so proud of Meg for putting her faith into practice. But there have certainly been times when she has shared how difficult it is to balance the needs of work and family. This is especially true because she has to travel so often. She sometimes has a hard time moving on from a story that has weighed on her heart and mind. But she feels called to work in this industry, bridge family and work, and try to inspire others.

If you have children who want to pursue big careers and dreams, my advice is this: the entertainment field is like a never-ending marathon. You think you are crossing the finish line, and then another twenty-six miles appear to test your faith. Paul encouraged us in 2 Timothy 4:7 with his example: "I have fought the good fight, I have finished the race, and I have kept the faith" (NIV).

—Richard and Mary Shrader, Megan's mom and dad

Two
My Journey
Small Steps Help Defining Moments
Become Fulfilled Dreams

I WAS BLESSED TO BE raised by parents, coaches, and teachers who told me I could be anything I wanted if I just worked hard enough. I realize now what a priceless gift of confidence that was. Two stories stand out in my mind as a result of that gift. The first took place when I was a sophomore in high school and had decided to run for class treasurer. I was standing in the kitchen and sharing my goal with my father. He listened and then politely said, "Why not president?" I thought about it for a moment, then asked myself, *Yeah! Why not president?* This was one of countless times when my parents would challenge me to dream bigger. I did run for president, and I won.

The second story that defines this mentality of being a strong female took place on the soccer field. I started playing when I was about five years old. When I was around ten or eleven, our coach began determining which positions we would settle into. Instead of rotating around to every position in every game, we began playing the same position all the time and perfecting that role on the team. It was decided I would play midfield. At this point in our level of play, it was pretty typical that the forwards would score all the goals and the midfield and defense positions would assist. But one game, when I was standing on the sidelines at halftime taking a drink from my water bottle, my coach pulled me aside and said, "Hey, Meg! I want you to start trying to score a goal from midfield. You have a great foot. I know you can kick the ball far. Start trying! I think you can make it!"

I stood there for a moment and thought, *Wait . . . me score a goal? From the middle of the field? I am usually standing pretty far away from the goal. . . . Hmmm.* But I went out on the field and started trying. And you know what? One game, I eventually scored! My coach had planted the idea in my head. His words of encouragement had energized me to dream bigger and try harder than I thought was my place. This mentality would help me and inspire me to keep setting goals countless times later in life. Looking back now, I see those were the first of my "girl power" moments. Throughout my life this mind-set has proved incredibly valuable in helping me achieve my goals while maintaining my faith.

The Early Years

I was born in Seattle, Washington, the younger of two girls. My father has spent his entire career as a financial advisor. During my childhood years, my mother stayed home with my sister and me. Later she completed a master's degree in art history and worked at various jobs in the art and design industry.

I have happy memories from my childhood. My father coached my sports teams. I sang in the school choir and tried out for school plays. (Sometimes I got a part; sometimes I didn't.) My sister, Becky, and I loved to sing and put on our own plays—musicals were our favorite—for my parents. To this day, Becky has one of the most beautiful singing voices I have ever heard. She is also hysterically funny and our days were, and still are, filled with a lot of laughter. We both were encouraged to pursue our talents. I liked trying different activities and stepping out of my comfort zone. I always enjoyed life to the fullest. I was busy, always on the go, but I think that is one reason I stayed out of trouble. If I wanted to make the volleyball team, I needed a certain GPA. And if I wanted to get elected to student council, I needed to demonstrate leadership qualities and gain the respect of my peers. Besides, I wanted to be a good kid and a hard worker because I had dreams of getting into a good college and pursuing a career one day.

I have attended church since I can remember, and my parents always made faith a priority in our family. My parents were people who did less talking about their beliefs and more doing—they were quiet leaders in various ways. I observed my dad being just as friendly to the security guard at his building as he was to the CEO; he taught me to treat everyone equally. My mom talked to me about social situations in my school and who might be feeling left out, and she taught me how important it is to look for the "lonely person on the playground" and be aware of people around me who might be hurting.

Those conversations stick in my head still today. I think it's one reason I am so comfortable walking into a party or social situation by myself. I can still hear my mom saying "It's okay to sit by yourself on the playground sometimes. You just might meet a friend you would otherwise not meet. Be available. Be accessible."

I remember asking Jesus into my heart in kindergarten and then making my own declaration in seventh grade at a summer camp. I had been following my parents' faith until then, but at that point I was ready to claim my faith for myself. I had been sprinkled with water, or christened, as a baby, but I owned it for myself in junior high. Right after college, when I was in my twenties, I decided to make a public profession of my faith again and was baptized in Nashville. I was just beginning my career, and I wanted to start my professional life with that act, with that public profession of my faith in Jesus. Being baptized seemed like a great way to begin my life as a business-woman.

I have never strayed from my faith. I knew in kindergarten, I knew as a teenager, I knew after I graduated from college, and today I still know Jesus as a personal Friend and my Savior, not just on Sunday, but every day. I have worshipped God with people in many different de-nominations. I was christened in an Episcopal church, attended youth group at a Nazarene church, got baptized in a Baptist church, and was married in a Methodist church! I also attended several nondenomina-tional churches in the various cities where I lived during my college years and early in my career. I appreciate all the beautiful and different ways we can worship God.

A Defining Moment

My parents decided to send my sister and me to one of the few Chris-tian schools in Seattle, and I attended King's Schools from kindergarten through high school. King's Schools gave me a priceless, well-rounded education. I was grounded academically, spiritually, socially, and pro-fessionally. Schoolwork and classes were tough, but my teachers were encouraging and creative. I attended chapel three times a week, and faith was woven into all our classes. Christianity wasn't forced on me; it was just a part of life. I loved school and dove in headfirst to many of the extracurricular activities offered there.

King's Schools belongs to a bigger organization called Crista Ministries, which also owns a radio station in Seattle called 105.3. My kindergarten teacher loves to tell this story about a day I vaguely re-member: our class took a field trip to the station. According to my teacher, when the class walked into the DJ booth and met the announcers, the station manager asked if anyone wanted to talk on the microphone. I didn't hesitate! I raised my hand and walked to the mic, where I proudly introduced myself and said—on the air—something to the effect of "I want to have this job someday!" When I hear this story, I think, *What a ham I was!* But that small moment had a big impact on my life. I was a little five-year-old, but dreams had already started forming for my life.

Perhaps you had a similar experience as a child—a defining moment that gave you a peek into the career you wanted to pursue. Moments like that are huge! Russell Wilson, quarterback for the Seattle Seahawks, recently wrote about his moment. As a high-school student, he'd attended Peyton Manning's football camp. Russell said that week of football and his interaction with an NFL quarterback had a profound impact on his career that began when he was drafted in 2012. Then, in 2014, Russell and the Seattle Seahawks played Peyton Manning and the Denver Broncos in Super Bowl 48 and won! I often wonder what that game was like for Russell, knowing he had such a defining moment with Peyton back in high school.

I often think of my defining moment—that radio station field trip—whenever I meet a child while I'm on the job. One time, for instance, when I was covering a 49ers vs. Seahawks game for CBS's *Thursday Night Football,* twin girls, about ten years old, came up to me and asked what it was like to be a news reporter. They explained they had been doing a lot of YouTube videos and their dad encouraged them to pursue their dreams of becoming newscasters. I loved being interviewed by them because I knew how they were feeling. This was an opportunity to pay it forward.

Life is full of defining moments. Look out for them and seize them!

Dreaming Big

When I was twelve years old, my parents got a flyer in the mail about a program called National American Miss. It was a pageant for young girls—but it wasn't at all like Miss USA or a TV pageant. Honest! There was no swimsuit contest, and the girls were not allowed to wear any makeup.

What I loved most about the competition—and this won't surprise you—was the speech portion. I got to talk into a microphone, and that excited me! One of the topics was My Favorite American. I had to write a speech that would be under two minutes, memorize it, and then deliver it from the stage. I chose Eleanor Roosevelt and talked about her leadership and service. I remember having so much fun putting the speech together and practicing. I worked on pausing for effect and delivering the last line with passion. I had so much fun that I wondered if I could give speeches for a living!

The second year I participated in the program, I won the title of Miss Washington Pre-Teen and, as a result, had some pretty cool experiences that year. I met the mayor of Seattle, sat in on a local newscast at the local TV station (you *know* I loved that!), and gave my Eleanor Roosevelt speech at a variety of venues, including a nursing home and the state fair. The pageant is now the largest youth pageant in the country, and I still emcee their events every summer.

Thinking back, I liked how the pageant got me to start dreaming big. When I prepared for the interview portion of the contest, for instance, I had to plan my answers to the following questions:

+ What do you want to study in college?

+ What career do you want to pursue?

+ What qualities do you look for in a friend?

✦ Who is your role model and why?

✦ How do you handle peer pressure?

Those were momentous questions for a thirteen-year-old, but pondering them helped me begin to formulate who I wanted to be and ignited my drive to succeed.

Around that time I started writing in a dream journal and would end each entry with my dreams and action points. While other girls were writing about their crushes, I was setting goals. I found some of my old journals recently and discovered some of the things I wrote:

1. Run for Student Council

2. Go on a missions trip

3. Make straight As

4. Get a part in the school play

5. Volunteer at the local museum

6. Get into accelerated classes to prepare for college

7. Practice your delivery as a newscaster

8. Be a news anchor

So the "make straight As" thing never really worked out—Math? Ugh!—but fueling the last two goals became a guidepost for me. I would watch Katie Couric on the *Today* show, Peter Jennings on ABC's *World News Tonight*, and Mary Hart on *Entertainment Tonight*. True to my goal number 7, I practiced my delivery by trying to copy theirs. And I even got my friends to join in. My friend Angela and I would create our own TV newscast and record it. My friend Sara and I would create our own radio show, complete with commercials, and record it on my tape recorder. And my best friend, Cindy Dondero, who is still my best friend, and I would film our own short home movies. They were so cheesy! But we had a blast. Cindy gets a kick out of watching me on television now because she knows that I wanted to do this since school. Those creative projects as a child are so important and were also a lot of fun.

By the time I was a freshman in high school, I was more than motivated to get good grades and start making this dream a reality. Also fueling that pursuit was a lesson my parents taught me: God gives all of us talents and how we use those talents is our gift to God. Even back then Ephesians 2:10 had an impact on me: "We are his workmanship, created in Christ Jesus for good works, which God prepared beforehand." I knew whatever I accomplished, I accomplished only because of a skill, talent, or opportunity God gave me—and He gave me those skills, talents, and opportunities so I could do good works for Him.

I began to seek out what those good works would be for me when I was in high school. What could I do to serve God? In what specific ways could I honor Him with my talents? These questions fueled my desire to set goals and achieve them. My high-school choir teacher, Mr. Pumphrey, was also instrumental in this quest. As a marathon runner, he set big goals for himself. He ran the Boston Marathon while I was in school, and he constantly challenged us to look at life as a race we were running for the Lord. Since choir was the very first class of the day, he started each class with a devotional reading. I still remember the day I first heard this verse: "I run with purpose in every step. I am not just shadowboxing. I discipline my body like an athlete, training it to do what it should. Otherwise, I fear that after preaching to others I myself might be disqualified" (1 Corinthians 9:26–27 NLT). This scripture solidified in my mind that the Lord wants us to approach life as though we are constantly training, striving to do better. And so I became even more serious about my goals and doing everything I could to reach them.

Let me mention, though, that while I enjoyed achieving my goals, I certainly failed at plenty. I lost the election for class president my senior year. I was cut from the basketball team my junior year. I nearly failed algebra as a sophomore. (I despise math—and I always will.) I also chopped off all my hair when I was a sophomore (Big mistake! Totally unflattering!) and got acne. But believe it or not, I was still happy. I enjoy life, and I always have. I genuinely looked at life as a glass that is half full—I still do! Romans 8:28 is one of my favorite verses: "We know that God causes all things to work together for good to those who love God, to those who are called according to His purpose." I believe God uses even life's heartaches and disappointments to give us a reason to draw closer to Him, and to enable us to help others through their heartaches and disappointments.

I believe God wants us to live the way these few verses teach—which is what Mr. Pumphrey modeled. To live with confidence in God, determination to please Him, commitment to do our best, and trust that, in the end, God will work out what's best for us. But we MUST give it our best!

I do agree that being confident in yourself, your abilities, and your goals is important. I think we can apply this confidence to our lives as Christians. I believe God calls us to do this.

A Postscript to High School

Last year I had the opportunity to visit my high school and speak to the students during a chapel service. As I was waiting backstage, I spotted some of my former teachers. When Miss Amble, my freshman Bible teacher, caught my eye, I raced over to her, put my hands on her shoulders, and said, "Never doubt that you are making a huge difference in these students' lives. I often think about words you shared and stories you told and about your fierce commitment to the Bible and to living life according to God's teaching. Your class was not easy, but it was so important and so life changing! I see that now. All those Bible stories and all those Bible verses I memorized have stayed with me all these years." At first Miss Amble looked a little surprised. Then she smiled, gave me a hug, and simply said, "Thank you." She shared that my words meant a lot to her and that she was proud of me and all I had accomplished.

Do you have a teacher who inspired you? If you are sitting in their classroom right now, drink up those moments. If those days are behind you, what can you do to thank them? What specific details will you share about how he or she encouraged you? Teachers are unsung heroes in our society; they shape the lives and characters of their students in priceless ways.

Not Always Easy

Even though I had a pretty great childhood, I also knew some rough patches growing up.

I had a fairly lonely eighth-grade year. Several times I ate lunch by myself either in the bathroom or outside as I hid behind a building. I had many acquaintances but few good friends. I didn't really belong to any certain group, and I was watching girls and boys start to date (if you want to call it that because no one could drive, so going on a date meant having your parents take you somewhere). I just wasn't into that. Eighth grade was also a time of lots of gossip and hurt feelings. I dealt with all that drama by walking around alone. I didn't want to participate, so I just kept to myself. But I believe this may have caused other students to think I was stuck-up and a goody-goody. Although I was a bit of a loner, I still had a great friend in Cindy and a few others.

Sometimes all you need is a few good friends! I was fortunate to have those and still, to this day, would rather have a few close friends who really know me.

At my high school, basketball was *the* sport. I played on the junior varsity team my freshman and sophomore years, but when I tried out for the varsity team, I didn't make it. I was really sad. I remember the coach calling me into his office and being very nice. He said something like, "I'm sorry, but it's just not going to happen this year." Some of my dear friends made the varsity team. I cried. I asked God, *Why?* And I was sure my life was over.

But soon I learned to activate what I now call "keeping my mind in a constant state of opportunity, in a constant state of what could be." I went home and told my parents the news. They let me cry for a few minutes and empathized with me. They knew I wanted to earn a varsity letter in a high school sport. I had always figured I'd letter in basketball, but getting cut ended that option. Then, not letting me sulk too long, my dad said his favorite phrase: "There is always something around the corner." And before long my creative juices started flowing again and I began thinking outside the box. I started to try to figure out what that something might be.

I had played volleyball in junior high and remembered enjoying it. So at the end of my sophomore year, when I knew I wouldn't be playing basketball the next year, I tossed around the idea of trying out for the volleyball team. I attended a volleyball camp that summer and played beach volleyball whenever I could. When it came time to try out for the team in the fall, I did my best—and I made the team! Talk about God closing a door and opening a window. To be totally blunt, our team was awful in terms of skill. I think we had the school's worst record ever at the end of the season, but we had a blast, and I really enjoyed the experience. And I learned something about what is valuable in life. My volleyball season was not a time of headliner victories or amazing achievements, but the experiences and friendships were life affirming and life shaping. I still remember things my coach said to us during practice. He used to kick things off with a quote. My favorite was "Attitude is the mind's paintbrush; it can color any situation." I realized then that experiences and relationships are often more significant than mere achievements.

I had my fair share of embarrassing moments. As I've mentioned, I cut my hair into a bob that was hideous, and I had a rough case of acne. When it didn't clear up with over-the-counter treatments, I visited a dermatologist and got a prescription for Accutane. If you have ever been on this medication, you know it really dries out your skin. So while my acne soon cleared up, my skin became very flaky and dry.

And while I was taking this medication, I made the mistake of going to get my eyebrows waxed. I had scheduled the appointment for the morning of prom. As I lay down on the table, they never asked me if I was on any medication. (These days most places ask, but this was a cheap nail salon in the 1990s.) Thanks to the Accutane, when they pulled off the wax, off came the skin right under my eyebrows! It . . . hurt . . . so . . . bad! I had never been waxed before, so I just thought it was supposed to hurt like crazy. But it continued to hurt as we drove home, and my eyebrows were still red and puffy and stinging an hour later. Well, I was wearing a red dress that night, so I gave my prom attire a 1950s theme. In an attempt to cover up my red, puffy eyebrows, I put on white cat-eye sunglasses and wore them the whole night. Luckily, a lot of my friends, including my date, thought I was just being bold with red eye shadow. We laughed! Laughter really is the best medicine, and I am thankful I had some good friends, and a wonderful date, to laugh with! My date, Tim Johnson, is still a good friend today. He works in Hollywood and is shining his own light.

Which Group? What Boundaries?

During high school we all figure out if we are going to join the fast crowd and party or be a jock, bookworm, theater kid, or youth-group kid. I was never in one group, though. I played basketball and volleyball, so I was a bit of jock. I tried to be a good student, which made me a bookworm, too. And I was also invited to some of those fast-crowd parties. I never drank, did drugs, or got involved with guys. If and when someone brought alcohol, I knew that was my cue to exit. Thankfully, I was never at a high school party where there was alcohol, but I certainly heard about those parties. I was also as careful as possible about who would be at the parties and what kind of environment I'd be in.

The toughest issue I ran into was R-rated movies. I remember one party when someone brought the DVD *Fear* with Reese Witherspoon and Mark Wahlberg. Since it was rated R, I knew it was time for me to leave, and I did. I remember a guy snickering at me as I walked out the door, but I didn't care. I didn't make a big deal out of skipping the movie. I just quietly gathered up my purse and coat and left. And it was easy for me to leave because I had decided before I ever went to a single party what I would or would not watch just as I had decided that I would leave immediately if alcohol appeared. Whenever I could, I drove myself to those parties so I knew I wasn't reliant on a friend who might want to stay longer than I did.

And if I didn't drive on a particular night, my parents and my older sister were really good about being just a phone call away. They never hesitated to pick me up when I asked them to. They didn't try to talk me out of going, because they knew I would choose wisely. We had previously talked about the standards in our family and they were understood. They just wanted me to know they were available if I needed them. I am so grateful for this approach. I firmly believe you need to decide what is right for you, for your faith, and for your family.

Talk about it! My parents were more than okay with the arrangement I just described, and I greatly valued their opinions.

Knowing when to leave and being clear about my boundaries continue to serve me well even today. When, for instance, work colleagues want to go out for drinks after work, I will usually go and join the conversation for a while. But whenever the group decides to move on to another bar or get another round of drinks, I know it's time for me to leave. I know my limit. When I sense the people or the drinking starting to get out of hand, I simply leave.

One time when I was a news anchor in San Antonio, a large group of the station on-air talent attended a charity ball. Our boss got drinks for the table. We had a few appetizers and enjoyed the evening and had some good laughs. Then, as the event wrapped up, our boss invited everyone out to a bar for another round of drinks. It was almost midnight. My husband (my boyfriend at the time) and I politely declined, thanked everyone for a great evening, and headed out. I was the only on-air talent who had declined. As I left, one of the other news anchors knowingly whispered in my ear, "You never say no to your boss!"

On the drive home I questioned whether I should have left the party or if I should have headed to a bar with my coworkers. I soon found out details about the evening that made me thankful I'd left when I had. It sounded like things eventually got a little out of hand. What great reinforcement for trusting both my gut and my decisions! But one of my coworkers who did stay actually said to me that week, "Why did you say no when our boss was asking us all to join him at the next bar?" I explained that, yes, I knew the guideline to never say no to your boss but chose not to follow it. I added that our boss did not treat me any differently for not joining him at the other bar. Who knows, maybe he even respected me more because of that decision.

Again, each one of us needs to determine what behaviors and boundaries are in line with our faith's guidelines and right for us. Establish your boundaries before you are in the situation you are preparing for—and then stick to them. Having your boundaries predetermined and in place will make it a lot easier to make a decision when faced with a situation at work or in life.

Overall, I am very thankful for my high school experience. I had some incredible teachers and coaches, many wonderful friends, and some pretty incredible experiences. I really tried to make the most of every opportunity. I had friends from all social circles and keep in touch with many of them to this day. My junior and senior year I was part of a vocal performance group, or glee club, called Living Faith, and that's what I really tried to do in my own little way. Live out my faith. High School was foundational for what was to come.

An Unusual Decision

My career aspirations really came into focus when I headed to Westmont College in sunny Santa Barbara, California. One of the toughest Christian schools academically, my freshman year at Westmont was filled with lots of late-night studying. But I think I was ready for that challenge. I also really enjoyed moving out of state and meeting new people. As an incoming freshman, I took the leap of faith to sign up to be matched with two unknown roommates. Kelly, Lisa, and I were very different in many ways, but they became two of my dearest college friends, and we had many nights of uncontrollable laughter and fun. I am so glad I got out of my comfort zone and allowed God to match us up as roommates! My freshman and sophomore years were filled with happy memories and adventures.

As a junior, I studied at American University in DC for a semester—and that experience was electric for me. I studied foreign policy, interned for a United States senator, and listened to speeches by every type of policymaker imaginable. I lived in a dorm with students from all over the country, students who had big dreams like mine, several of whom were already leading in a big way. Some were student body president of their colleges; one was the debate club president. Many had been valedictorians of their high school classes. I was so inspired to be around them. When I realized student body elections were coming up at Westmont, I emailed the current student body president. I asked him if running from "abroad" was even possible. He said it was but that I needed to do two things: be present on campus to give my speech, and if I won the election, to return again in the spring to hire my council. My parents were supportive, but several friends thought I was crazy and worked hard to discourage me from running. Two other women had already declared their candidacy. Talk about girl power! Regardless of who won, it was a proud moment for Westmont: it would be the first time three women were running for student body president. But I still wasn't sure I was up to the task. I'll never forget the turning point for me.

I was walking the halls of American University and thinking about my decision. As I crossed one of the main gathering areas, I looked up and saw a large poster hanging from the banister of the staircase going up to the second floor. Scrawled in red paint was "Isaiah 6:8—Here I am, Lord. Send me." I stared at that Bible verse—on display at this secular campus—and my heart started beating fast. This was too coincidental. I had my answer.

I talked to some of my American University friends about my decision. They were excited for me and helped me map out a strategy. We decided that if I was going to do it, I needed to fly to my school on Tuesday to campaign for a few days before the election speech on Friday. Most students put up a few posters on campus and spread the word through their friends, but that approach would not work for me.

I was not physically present on campus for that entire spring semester; I needed to make the most of my few days on campus before I gave my speech.

What serendipity that I was currently studying and living at the nation's capital. I was watching politicians and think tanks and policy-makers—the best in the world—campaign! I had observed their persistence, their communication techniques, their passion, and their strategies. I was determined to apply these skills to my campaign.

An Unusual Campaign

One of my American University friends, the former student body vice president of Tulane University in New Orleans, gave me some valuable advice. "If you don't know where to start, do what Bill Clinton did: start knocking on doors." He told me when Clinton lost the race for governor of Arkansas in 1974, the very next day he was out knocking on doors and meeting people. The very next day! Despite the scandals surrounding Bill Clinton, I was impressed by his determination. George W. Bush has a similar story of determination when he set out to unseat popular Texas governor Ann Richards. It seems hustle (which I talk about in chapter 3) has no political party, because he also won.

So, when I arrived at Westmont College to give my campaign speech, what's the very first thing I did? I started knocking on doors. I was nervous, and I felt a little silly. But I wanted to win this election and serve my college. I had only three days to convince two thousand students I was the best candidate. I did not have a platform per se, but I believed through my time in Washington, DC, I gleaned ideas about how to bring fresh and positive change to my campus. Time was precious, but I had to start somewhere.

So I literally walked to the freshman dorm and knocked on doors. Sometimes students answered; sometimes they didn't. But when they did answer, I introduced myself, told them I was running for president, and said I would appreciate their votes. I asked what particular issues were important to them. A few shared some concerns and some asked me for specific ideas, but you know what the most common response was? "Wow! I'm a freshman. You're a junior. And I don't even know who the other candidates are. It's nice to put a face with a name." Many students added, "Thanks for asking my opinion. I don't usually care about student elections, but because you made the effort, I will show up and vote for you." I made my way through both of the freshman dorms that night. The next day I headed to the sophomore dorms and did the same thing. You know what? I had a blast. A few friends started out with me, but they quickly lost interest or got sidetracked, so I knocked on most doors alone.

"Some succeed because they are destined to, but most succeed because they are determined to (Henry Van Dyke)." I believe this wisdom, and I was determined. And along the way, I met some new friends I would not have normally met. One of the highlights of my senior year was seeing the underclassmen whose doors I had knocked on and chatted with during my short campaign. Because of my door-to-door campaign and the subsequent chitchat that ensued, we had an excuse to say hi to one another on campus.

To make a long story short, I won the election. Stan Gaede, who was president at the time and who is still a dear friend, sent me an email when I won. (It was customary for the current president of the college to invite the student body president-elect for coffee after the election, but he was off the hook, as I had flown back to DC already.) He told me he'd heard that people were shocked someone could pull off a long-distance campaign and an election-day victory. But when God wants you to succeed, He will make it happen. Inspired by the Isaiah banner I had seen hanging in the hall, I had committed that election to the Lord. I had prayed about the whole process—the strategy, the campaigning, the speaking—and then I worked like crazy to make it happen.

I returned to Westmont in the fall for my senior year, and my experience as student body president was priceless. It was interesting and exciting and stimulating, but it was also very hard. I had to make tough choices, and I learned what leadership skills I lacked. I discovered I don't lead meetings very well, and I had to deal with disappointing people. I learned I can't please everyone. Also, because I was in the public eye, I was sometimes the target of anger, frustration, and scorn. It came with the job.

At one point someone wrote an op-ed about me for the school paper, expressing disappointment in my choosing to promote one activity over another. The choice hadn't totally been mine. My vice president actually had more of a hand in the decision than I did, but as President Harry Truman said, "The buck stops here." As president, I was held responsible for all decisions made by my staff or me while I was in office. But that article still hurt. It was very public, and I felt wounded.

These experiences taught me priceless skills—such as learning how to communicate more effectively with my staff, handling conflict and complaints, and dealing with public opinions on my performance. TV viewers frequently email me at *Inside Edition* and express all kinds of opinions about my hair, my clothes, my voice, my mannerisms, and the story I covered. I need to have a thick skin, or else all that criticism would have me crying all the time. I think experiencing a bit of disapproval as student body president helped prepare me to cope with my critics and learn you can't please everyone.

Overall, serving as student body president at Westmont was a terrific experience. I wouldn't trade it for the world. It taught me valuable life skills that guide me in my career to this day.

Takeaway

1. Bad haircuts and acne will pass! Everyone goes through rough patches. Keep your chin up!

2. Set your boundaries before you are faced with a difficult situation.

3. Make yourself available. Be willing to serve.

4. When faced with a daunting and seemingly impossible task (campaigning in three days, for instance), approach the problem creatively and enthusiastically. Pray hard, work hard, and you might be surprised what you can accomplish. Even if you fail, you will have experienced the process and grown from it.

5. When you have a big task and aren't sure where to start, knock on doors. Start meeting and talking to people, and clearly state what you are doing. Even if I had not won the election for student-body president, I would still have met freshmen and sophomores I'd never have met otherwise.

6. Appreciate and recognize that people in positions of leadership—and in life—can't please everyone. All you can do is your very best and learn from it.

*F*ew people understand the constant hustle in the entertainment business. It's not for the faint of heart. When I first began on this crazy journey in the industry, it was easy to get distracted by any- and everything—and it still is. To be successful, I found that you must have a strong work ethic, a great team supporting you, unstoppable energy, and unwavering faith. I had to intentionally set guidelines on what family time would look like next to the constant city-to-city touring and travel. I love what I've been called to do, but even today, now as a grandfather, I am constantly juggling work, family, friends, and creative projects.

In this chapter, Megan shares the joys and struggles of constant red-eye flights, life on the road, and deadlines. It is called "hustle," and that is what you need if you want to really thrive in this industry. I think it is important to speak candidly and honestly about the sacrifices that will often be required. But the blessings that unfold will far overshadow those hard days and sleep-deprived nights!

—Michael W. Smith, Grammy award–winning singer,
songwriter, producer

Three

Do the Hustle

What's the Key to Success?

> ***Don't be upset with the results
> you didn't get by the work you didn't do.***
>
> —UNKNOWN

JUST TALKED ABOUT THE HUSTLE involved with running for student government in college. But what about the workplace? What does that look like? What are the keys to success in the entertainment industry—or any industry? Let me start with a couple of quotes that have shaped my journey and motivated me over the years:

> *"Whatever your hand finds to do, do it with all your might."*
> (Ecclesiastes 9:10 RSV)

> *"Let us run the race with perseverance the race marked out for us."*
> (Hebrews 12:1 NIV)

So how do we do what these verses suggest? How do we work "with all our might"? I think in a practical term, it means HUSTLE.

Hustle Defined

I get so excited when someone I admire releases a book. Why? Because it offers valuable glimpses into his or her life. In those pages are opportunities to glean insight about that person's triumphs, mistakes, victories, and adventures. My dad always encouraged me to read as I was growing up, and I think reading helped prepare me for my career and for life in general as much as college and internships did. And even as I prepared to write this book, I read as many books by successful people as I could.

I noticed a common theme in all of them: all successful people seem to have that fire in the belly, that burning desire to reach a goal no matter what the cost. Can this kind of passion be taught? Or is it something you are born with? Maybe it's a little of both. Whatever their natural level of passion, though, all successful people hustle.

In Ivanka Trump's book *The Trump Card: Playing to Win in Work and Life*, she shares that a key to her success has been going in early to work. She and her two brothers learned this from their father. They like to be the first ones in the office every morning and the last ones to leave. She thinks this communicates a good message to all their employees: everyone is there to work hard, including the top brass. I see this as hustle.

In her excellent book *Making the Case: How to Be Your Own Best Advocate*, Kimberly Guilfoyle, a legal analyst at Fox News, shared that when she wanted to get into TV and host her own show, she did not wait for the deal to come to her. She flew to New York City, walked into the Court TV studios, found the person who was hiring, and stated why she would be a great host. She got the job. Some would call that being pretty forward and bold. I call that hustle.

First Impressions Only Happen Once

Many people do not understand hustle.

A friend of mine recently bought a condo. A busy woman, she needed some help decorating and moving her furniture into the place. So she found the name of a gal recently out of college who was looking for a job. My friend invited her to a lunch meeting to discuss hiring her as a part-time interior decorator. Do you know how this millennial responded? "Well, I have hot yoga at noon, but I could meet you afterward, at two o'clock."

When I heard this story, my jaw hit the floor. I'm sorry, but did you say you wanted a job? Do you want to be able to pay for your hot yoga classes? My parents taught me to jump when a job opportunity came my way. You've probably heard the expression "You never get a second chance to make a first impression." That young woman made a very poor first impression. Needless to say, she did not get the job, but she offers an important lesson. I believe you jump on the first call from a potential employer or you get forgotten. And you don't stop jumping once you get the job.

I learned quickly that in the world of entertainment and media, you rarely get to set your own schedule. That's because TV shows and film sets require hundreds of people who work all hours. Your call time might be inconvenient, like 4:30 a.m. So if you decide you'd rather not get up that early and instead call in sick, you are not just calling in sick to a supervisor. You are instead advertising your lack of interest to many people, and you may be affecting an entire scene, story, or broadcast. You won't be told, "Sure! Let us know how you feel tomorrow." You will probably be demoted or even fired.

Some of the most successful people in Hollywood and the media are also the hardest workers. The general public often has no idea what goes into making and producing TV shows, films, and broadcasts.

Like many high school students, when I thought about my first job in the entertainment industry, I actually assumed I would have a nine-to-five job, then get invited for dinner, get to celebrate every holiday, and take great vacations—and that if I auditioned for an acting job, I would get it on the second or third try. Boy, was I wrong! I quickly learned that if I wanted to make it in the entertainment/media business, I had to be flexible, adaptable, passionate, committed, and resilient. I realized I also needed to hustle and keep hustling.

Let me give you a few examples of the hustle I needed—and that you need—to succeed.

Striving for Success

As I've mentioned, I participated in a National American Miss pageant when I was twelve years old, and it was a great experience for me. When I was eighteen, I was asked to host one of these pageants. It was a fun summer job while I pursued my television career via college and internships. The shows were held on weekends, and at one point I was hosting weekend shows in about ten different states. As the host, I got to sharpen my announcer skills, travel the country, and get a paycheck.

After I earned my degree, it took a while and several part-time jobs, but I eventually got my break in television: morning traffic anchor at a news show in San Antonio. My shift was from 5:00 a.m. to 10 a.m. I was, however, still trying to emcee a few pageants when I could. In fact, when I got the job, I had just agreed to emcee a show on Thanksgiving Day at Disneyland. But my anchor job required me to be on the air in Texas the very next morning at 5:00 a.m. Yikes!

What did I do? I ended up walking off the stage after the pageant in California, getting into a car with my suitcase, driving straight to the airport in my evening gown, taking a red-eye flight to San Antonio, arriving at 3 a.m., driving to the station, changing into a business suit, and anchoring the news at five o'clock. Whew! Why? you ask. Why do that? Because I believed I should honor my previous commitments, and I also believed hustling would pay off. And I keep hustling even though I'm years into my career and have a steady job. As I write this chapter, I have flown from Nashville to New York City for work at *Inside Edition*, to San Jose to give a speech at a prayer breakfast, then on to Las Vegas to cover the Academy of Country Music Awards, and finally onto a red-eye flight back to New York—all within a matter of five days. I am battling a cold and very tired. But I made commitments to people and businesses in all those states that I needed to fulfill. Plus, I love what I do. I love to "run with perseverance the race" as stated in Hebrews 12:1 NIV. One could say I'm kinda addicted to it! I love meeting a challenge with hustle.

Keep Moving

Even after I became a full-time news anchor, I still looked for ways to get involved in other aspects of my industry. After all, my stockbroker father had always warned my sister and me not to put all our eggs in one basket. I was paying the bills as a broadcaster, but I still wanted to tap into my other talents. I wanted to learn all the different ways the media and entertainment world impacts culture and business, as well as all the players involved. Beyond just journalism, I wanted to tap into the creative aspects of my personality and pursue jobs in that area. Just as the people I admired were always actively moving forward on projects, I also had a strong desire to keep achieving, keep moving, keep going! I equate it with this quote by hotel mogul Conrad Hilton: "Success seems to be connected with action. Successful people keep moving. They make mistakes, but they don't quit."

One of the more interesting and fulfilling parts of the entertainment industry for me is acting. And acting is not for the faint of heart.

Why? Because it is all about rejection! I'm just being honest. I have auditioned for acting parts for over a decade, and 99 percent of the time I haven't gotten the role. If I were in it to pay the bills, I would be homeless. It's just too competitive an industry for many people to be able to make a living at it.

But every once in a while, just when I think I should give up, I get that magical phone call from my agent. "Megan, you got the part!" This was the case with the movie *Redeemed*. I auditioned for the part with the producer in Hollywood via Skype. The audition required me to cry, and that was hard. When my agent called to share the wonderful news, I started thinking about the tricky part: we would be shooting in Los Angeles, but I live in Nashville and I work in New York.

So I *hustled*. I flew to NYC from Nashville on Sunday morning, covered the MTV Movie Awards for *Inside Edition* that night in Brooklyn, drove to the airport, jumped on a red-eye flight to LA, landed at 4 a.m., rented a car, slept for a few hours in my car, headed to the movie set for an 8 a.m. call time, filmed the movie all day Monday, worked Tuesday in LA from our *Inside Edition* office there, returned to filming the movie Wednesday, and that night took a red-eye home and landed in Nashville at 8 a.m.

Why? Because that was the only way to make it happen. Did I need a nap on Saturday after those two red-eye flights in the same week? You better believe it! But it was well worth the effort. As I've mentioned, if you want to achieve your dreams and goals, whatever the industry you're working in, you need to be willing to give up sleep, rearrange your schedule, and make sacrifices. Very often, the result will be a juggling act that is not for the timid. Another case in point . . .

On season 2 of the ABC drama *Nashville*, I was cast in a small role as a fictional news reporter. I got the part after a long process. I must have auditioned a dozen times. My great acting agent faithfully booked audition after audition and developed a good relationship with the casting agent. So I just kept trying.

On another front, CBS had hired me as special correspondent to cover its eight *Thursday Night Football* games and give reports for all the local CBS affiliates across the country. Our first game was early September in Baltimore. It was a big deal, and not only because it was our first. The Ray Rice scandal (he assaulted his girlfriend) had just broken, he had been kicked off the team, and it was one of the top stories of the moment.

So there I was, prepping for this football game when, on Tuesday, my acting agent called and told me I had won the role of a reporter on *Nashville.* Then she dropped the bombshell: the show taped on Friday at 9 a.m.! (You often learn just a few days before or sometimes as late as the night before that you have booked a role on a TV show. Movies often book people further in advance.) So I quickly determined what I needed to do.

I would fly to Baltimore on Wednesday night, prep for the game, go live on air on Thursday at 4:00, watch the game, go back on air at 11 p.m., and give postgame reports until 1:30 a.m. Then I'd dash back to my hotel, get a few hours of sleep, jump in my car at 4:30, catch a 6 a.m. flight back to Nashville, and be on the set at 9:00. I'd tape my episode until about 3:00, wrap, and head home to see my family. Schedules like that make me very prayerful: *Lord, may my flights not be delayed!*

This is a realistic example of how life will look if you want to do it all. You won't always get to plan your schedule. You won't necessarily even know your schedule very far in advance. You will be obligated to other people—to do what they want you to do when and where they want you to do it. And, no, they will not wait for you. Just know that if you want a full life of marriage, family, and career, be ready to make the necessary sacrifices—and do the necessary hustle. And for goodness' sake, when you are starting out, if an opportunity presents itself, skip the hot yoga class for one day and seize that opportunity!

Life Is Not a Party

From the start of my career, I have observed this truth again and again in my interactions with celebrities. Like so much of the public, I assumed that celebrities partied and relaxed between jobs. I quickly learned this was not the case. I cannot tell you how many times I have interviewed a celeb on the red carpet at an awards show, and the conversation goes something like this: "Hi, [Tim McGraw or Hugh Jackman]. You are nominated for several awards tonight and a favorite to win. How are you going to celebrate after the show?"

They say, "Oh, I don't have time to celebrate. I need to get on our tour bus and head to [city] for a concert tomorrow!" Or "Celebrate? I'm jumping on a red-eye tonight because our film [title] starts shooting tomorrow." Successful celebrities are still keeping rigorous schedules, giving up sleep, and making sacrifices in order to stay successful. Their work ethic is incredible.

And that is true about anyone who is successful. Whatever their line of work, these individuals jump at opportunities whenever they arise. They show up early and stay late. They follow up a job interview with a thank-you letter. They dress for the job they want. And when someone invites them to a meeting or job interview, they make a good impression by going above and beyond. They go the extra mile. They rise to the occasion.

And all those things are . . . hustle.

Great Hustlers in the Entertainment Field

Let me offer you a couple more examples of an impressive work ethic.

✦ I love the story I heard several years ago about Tyra Banks. When the first season of her talk show was just about to premiere, instead of sitting back and having other people do all the prep work, it was said that Tyra was up the night before with a hammer, nails, and some sequined decorations to make sure her set looked exactly the way she wanted it to. She was engaged and proactive—and those, too, are qualities of a leader. Tyra also studied her mentor, Oprah, and took time to learn the ins and outs of having her own talk show. Many would sit back and expect success to come to them, but Tyra got involved and did her homework. Tyra hustled.

✦ My talented friend Storme Warren is the host of the daily show called *The Highway* on SiriusXM radio. Not only is he talented, but Storme is known as the Dick Clark of country music because he is one of the nicest and most hardworking guys in the business. I met him when we both were hired to host the Inspirational Country Music Awards, and he told me an awesome story I won't forget that showed his work ethic. Storme told me about a time he accidentally double-booked himself. He had agreed to host a Little Big Town concert in East Tennessee as well as a Martina McBride charity concert in Nashville—both on the same night! The events were about a two-hour drive apart. He realized that even if he hit no traffic, he wouldn't make it. But he had made both commitments, and he didn't want to have to choose between the two.

As he tried to figure out what he could do, a friend jok-
ingly suggested he take a helicopter from one event to the
other. Storme immediately contacted a helicopter company
in Nashville, explained the situation, and offered to give the
company free press on his radio show and all night at both
events. You know what? The helicopter company agreed and
Storme pulled it off. He actually hosted both events that
night, thanks to a fast helicopter ride, his resourceful friend,
and his refusal not to give up until he had a solution. Some
people think this story is crazy, but I love it. It made such
an impression on me because it shows what persistence and
hard work look like. I believe Storme is one of the best country music radio hosts, not only because of his talent, but because he is willing to hustle.

✦ When I need a little inspiration, I follow the Rock (Dwayne
Johnson) on Instagram. He is one of the hardest-working
guys I know in the entertainment industry. As I write this
book, he has 23 million followers on Instagram and 50 million
on Facebook. One of his favorite hashtags is #HardestWorker
IntheRoom. He is extremely disciplined with his time. His
alarm clock frequently goes off at 4:30 a.m., and he posts a
picture to prove it before he dashes off to the gym or jumps
on a flight across the country. He sticks to an incredibly strict
diet for certain movie roles, and he is constantly thanking
his fans for supporting his projects. He frequently mentions
how important it is to have a good team around you, his team
being his agent, manager, personal trainer, business partners,
friends, and family.

But Dwayne's secret to success lies in his determination to
work hard even when no one is watching. He recently posted

his answer to the question, "What is the key to success?" I think his reply is spot-on: "One of the things is the willingness to put in the hard work . . . when you're alone. Everyone works hard when eyes are on them. Boss watching, teachers, trainers, coworkers, etc. Pushing yourself past your limits and working extremely hard when no one is watching is what makes all the difference in the world and sets you up for success."

I do believe God wants us to hustle. He wants this kind of commitment from us. Far too many Christians sit back, pray about what they want to do, and then just wait for things to happen. This approach to life or a career rarely, if ever, works, and it definitely doesn't honor our Savior. What does honor God is working hard, using the gifts He has given you, going where He calls you, taking steps of faith when He requires them, and, yes, hustling! I truly believe that when you do these things, God will reward you. It's a promise: "You will enjoy the fruit of your labor. How joyful and prosperous you will be!" (Psalm 128:2 NLT).

Takeaway

1. Successful people have that fire in the belly. They are willing to go the extra mile.

2. Hustling hard will pay off, because you will stand out in a crowd. Most people give up when the going gets tough.

3. Very successful people are often the hardest workers in the room. They are not partying as much as we think.

4. Our hard work can be a way to honor God.

I've been fortunate enough to be a working professional in the entertainment industry for almost two decades. When chatting on set in Mumbai, India, for our upcoming film *Heartbeats,* I shared with Megan that I began as a screenwriter. Then, as I segued into directing a few years back, I realized there is no set "alumni network" in Hollywood for directors; there is no regular group that meets on Wednesday nights to share trade secrets with those of us cutting our teeth. I needed some insider tips, so I sought out the wisdom of several screenwriters-turned-directors whose work I admired. These mentors were gracious with their time and generous in sharing their experiences and offering advice. This sharing was invaluable to me and made me feel more confident about prepping a film, collaborating with talent and department heads, and keeping my feet light by changing socks at lunch. (As a director, I'm on those feet all day, and changing socks at lunch truly *was* one of the best tips I received.)

When seeking a mentor, we shouldn't look for someone who will show us how to do our job; we can only truly learn that from experience. Instead, what we should look for is someone who will share with us practical nuts-and-bolts advice, the kind of working tips people know only if they've worn the same hat we are about to put on. All we need to do, then, is bring an open mind and open ears—and afterward offer a heartfelt thank-you to those mentors for sharing with us.

—Duane Adler, screenwriter of films *Step Up, Save the Last Dance*, and screenwriter and director of *Heartbeats*

Four

Mentors

Who Doesn't Need Wisdom, Friendship, and Encouragement?

A mentor is someone who allows you to see the hope inside yourself.

—OPRAH

OW DID YOU DO IT?" people often ask my parents. "How did you raise a daughter who managed to stay out of trouble and is now a successful professional?" Parents also approach me and ask, "What caused you to choose the right roads and behavior?" Several things, but I think one of the most powerful influences is the people we hang around. Whom we spend our time with has a huge impact on our decisions and experiences. I know this has been the case with me. One of the most important factors in keeping me on a good path is the mentors I've been blessed to have along the way. When I think of my mentors, I'm reminded of Proverbs 27:17: "As iron sharpens iron, so one person sharpens another (NIV)." Mentors are people I admire, people I want to be around, and people I strive to be like. When we were young, my dad would tell my sister and me, "Show me your friends, and I'll show you your future."

Meet Rebekah

I have always had someone to look up to, someone a few years older and more experienced who helped keep me motivated to do the right thing. Someone whose life I wanted to emulate. I know that following another person's positive example was key to keeping me on the straight and narrow path. These mentors and role models kept me motivated, and that's still true today. I am blessed to have mentors who inspire me, encourage me, and sometimes pray for me. Having someone to respect and imitate is invaluable.

I was in high school when I found my first mentor. Rebekah Metteer was in the class ahead of mine. We played on the volleyball team together, and I admired how she lived her life. She got along easily with people of all ages and in all social circles, she earned fantastic grades, and she seemed to find the good in everyone and everything. I especially appreciated how she made it clear that her relationship with God was number one and how she was open about her decision to save sex for marriage. Rebekah also had a wicked sense of humor, was super talented, and lived life to the fullest. She modeled a lot of the qualities I wanted to be part of my own character.

So I made an effort to be around her. If Rebekah auditioned for the school play, I did, too. Rebekah was part of a singing group called Living Faith, so I joined. Yes, it sounds as if I were stalking her, but that's not the case! But I was intentional about being around her because I wanted her good qualities to rub off on me. I knew she was not only a good role model but also a good influence.

Rebekah was what I call "good people." At the time, I didn't refer to Rebekah formally as a mentor, but looking back I see that's exactly what she was to me. In fact, she started my lifelong pursuit of relationships with people I liked as role models. I knew the value of such mentors regardless of the season of my life or the stage of my career.

To this day Rebekah remains a good friend. Even though she is in Seattle and we rarely see each other, we keep up on Facebook, and I continue to learn from her from afar.

Rebekah is a precious example of one kind of mentor: she was similar to a big sister, she was a good Christian friend, and she was a much-appreciated encourager. But as my life unfolded and I found myself in different situations and new work environments, I realized what a wide range of mentoring is possible. We miss out on important relationships if, for instance, we think mentors just offer career advice or only discuss spiritual matters. Mentors can share valuable wisdom and life-giving friendship for every season of life.

When I worked as a news anchor in San Antonio, I found mentors in both my personal and professional lives. Personally, through friends in my church, I found a female mentor in a wonderful lady named Raelyn. She was a chaplain and led a Bible study in her home for young women in their twenties. And professionally, I found a mentor in the sales manager at my TV station. Sara Fulmer inspired me by how she treated her clients. I would often interact with Sara due to my role as a cohost on *Great Day SA*. I got to witness her warm interactions with clients and appreciated how seriously she took their businesses. She taught me how to really listen while on a story. As reporters, we are often fighting deadlines and are super busy. But Sara managed to make sure all the people who were featured in our stories felt appreciated and listened to. Listening to someone is a huge gift. Sara was a mentor in this way, and to this day I still think of her when I begin a new assignment and meet the interview subjects for the first time. Raelyn and Sara were two very different mentors, but both taught me equally valuable skills.

Distant Mentors

We can also admire and glean wisdom from people we may never meet. Sheryl Sandberg, Brené Brown, Condoleezza Rice, Megyn Kelly, and Oprah—I watch, learn from, and greatly admire these women. In fact, I consider them my distant mentors. I have met some of these women briefly. I don't have a relationship with any of them, yet their influence in my life is vital. Sheryl Sandberg is COO of Facebook and one of the leading female tech executives today. She is making decisions that affect anyone who uses these life-changing technologies, and empowering women to take more leadership roles in business. Brené Brown writes about being authentic and taking risks in life. When I read her books, I feel like I am getting a therapy session with her. I respect Condoleezza Rice, former secretary of state, and Megyn Kelly, Fox News anchor, for their strong leadership and commanding presence. It was so inspiring to see Condoleezza negotiate with world leaders, and Megyn Kelly boldly asked intelligent, important questions when she interviewed presidential candidates on her primetime TV show, which often led to a passionate debate where she more than confidently held her own. And I consider it my own personal workshop to watch Oprah Winfrey's Super Soul Sunday on her OWN network and observe this powerful billionaire be completely vulnerable as she reveals the private side of her life and chats with notable psychologists and authors about family, faith, and overcoming hardships. Just watching and observing these distant mentors inspires me to work harder in my life and dream bigger.

Technology and the internet allow us access to the teaching and wisdom of distant mentors like never before. Think about your distant mentors. Who's on your list?

Casual Mentors

And if you don't have any mentor relationships on the horizon, don't worry! Casual mentors can be just as influential, and not as intimidating to approach. In her bestselling book *Lean In: Women, Work, and the Will to Lead*, Sheryl Sandberg shares an interesting insight about how to set up mentor relationships and how not to. She tells about the awkwardness she felt when young professionals would approach her and say, "Hi! Will you be my mentor?" This approach does not always work. Sheryl stated it can seem forced and makes her uncomfortable. She prefers that mentoring come about more organically and naturally. When, for example, two people are already in the same department and working on a project together, the conversation is easier. That proximity also ensures your paths will cross regularly, helping your mentor understand your particular circumstances in context. Most of the time, a mentor-mentee relationship should grow out of some commonality rather than a blind-date sort of arrangement. I call these people casual mentors: less pressure, and they are often all around you!

If you're looking for a casual mentor, consider people you often come in contact with. Do you work in the same office or at least the same industry? Being in a shared space allows you to glean wisdom from people who are your casual mentors.

Deborah Norville, the anchor of *Inside Edition*, is one of my casual mentors. We don't have official once-a-month meetings to go out for coffee and talk, but I've come to really value our five-minute conversations in the makeup room or studio hallway. Every so often, while I'm getting ready for an interview or covering a story, she will ask how it's going. I answer but then quickly shift the conversation by asking, "And what do you think of . . . ?" I love to ask her opinion. Deborah has had a long and diverse career in the television world, she is well traveled and well educated, so she always has an interesting perspective on whatever I bring up. Occasionally I'll ask her about a topic outside our industry, perhaps about her marriage, her family, or her faith. She has been married to the same man for more than twenty-five years and has raised three kids while balancing a demanding career, writing books, speaking, and volunteering in support of veterans—and I like learning how she does it five-minute conversation by five-minute conversation.

Another of my casual mentors is a female motivational speaker at my church in New York named Lynette Lewis. Lynette flies in and out of the city frequently because her husband leads two different churches—one in Raleigh, North Carolina, and our church in New York City. A former corporate executive, today Lynette is an author, speaker, avid runner, and mom of twins! Through my involvement in some women's groups at our church, I have been fortunate to draw wisdom and advice from her. Lynette has taught me to make new friends in all circumstances because relationships make life richer and more fulfilling. She has encouraged me to be bold in setting and achieving goals and told me to be proud of the bold personal decisions I have made as a believer. She has also challenged me and countless others to be on the lookout for ways to encourage people to be the best they can be.

One more thing: as you recognize casual mentors in your life, not only will you develop lasting friendships and learn about how to have a more productive life and career, you might also see doors of opportunity open for you. During church activities and Bible studies, Lynette would frequently connect me with other like-minded individuals in New York City. I have developed many new relationships and business contacts because of her, and some of those have led to fulfilling business opportunities.

Personal Mentors

Of course, we also need personal mentors who get to know all aspects of your life—not just your professional side but also how you are doing spiritually, relationally, and emotionally. These are the mentors you do meet with on a regular basis.

When I was student body president at Westmont College, I had the privilege of meeting with the school president, Stan Gaede, every other week, which is when he invited me to his office for a thirty-minute coffee chat. We tended to focus on the student body and any issues the students were facing, but he also asked about me: How did I feel about leading a team? How was my course load? What career was I pursuing? What spiritual issues was I facing? These chats were invaluable on so many levels.

Along the way, Stan gave me his best advice for leadership: get to know your team both professionally and personally. Stan met weekly with a council of eight administrative officials. He kept a notecard at his desk listing their first names. His goal was to touch base with each of them individually at least every other week to talk about something non-work related. He asked how family members were doing, about the person's golf game, what books they were reading, or plans for their next family vacation. Once he touched base with a person, he put a checkmark next to the name on the notecard. After he had checked every name on the card, he threw that card away and started fresh with a new notecard. That remarkable example taught me the importance of developing authentic and quality relationships with my coworkers. I often think of Stan's strategy and do my best to adapt it for my own workplace.

On an even more intimate level, my mom is my personal mentor. She has been my best friend since I was born, and I owe so much of my success to her. I have watched her raise two confident daughters, maintain a loving marriage of forty-three years and counting, pursue her master's degree, take on a variety of jobs, care for her parents, and be an extremely supportive aunt, cousin, mother-in-law, and grandmother. I admire her strength, her faith, and her firm commitment to her family. I can only pray I will be as good a mother and nana as she is.

Sometimes a family member can be a personal mentor, but that is not an option for everyone. Still, personal mentors can be found. Pray and ask God to provide you with one. Look around and be open to whom He might put into your life to take on that role. After all, family doesn't happen only by blood or marriage. Sometimes what starts as a more casual mentor relationship will deepen into a personal mentorship. Maybe a weekly walk with a neighbor you admire or a monthly lunch date with a more experienced colleague will offer the heart connection and relationship you're seeking. Make time for these connections. Such relationships are life affirming and life enriching.

Be the Mentor!

At some point it will be your turn to mentor someone. You may not consider yourself ready or prepared, but someone will look to you for advice. And before you know it, *you* will be the one handing out wisdom. It happened that way for me a few years ago. Out of the blue, my friend Amira called and asked if I would be willing to mentor a fresh-out-of-college twentysomething named Keeley, who had just moved to New York City to pursue acting, modeling, and working for a campus ministry. Amira knew a bit about my story and thought we would be a great match. I was asked if I would agree to the more formal arrangement of meeting with her every month for six months.

I know from experience how easy it is to feel very lost and alone in the Big Apple because people are so busy. Still—and I'm being honest—I just wasn't sure I should or even could say yes. First, I was extremely busy working full-time as a reporter at *Inside Edition*. I was flying every week for work, had a husband and a new baby, and was trying to balance a social life and time with my family. Second, the connection felt a little forced. Commit to meet with a young woman I had never met—and commit to meet for six months? What if we

didn't click? Besides, what could I possibly offer her? I started doubt-
ing my value as a guide. What would we even talk about?

Looking back, I find it almost comical how apprehensive I was
about the situation. I hesitantly asked Amira about the structure of the
mentorship and what Keeley would expect of me. Amira reassured me
she had prayed about the match and felt strongly that I would be a great
fit for Keeley. Amira also explained that I would need to participate in a
training session, but I could do that on the phone. She then shared that
her hope was for us to meet once a month for a year. She said the most
important thing I could do was listen and just be a friend. Fears some-
what allayed, I prayed about the situation and knew I needed to do it. I
realized how much my mentors have meant to me, and I thought about
how scary it must be for Keeley to move to the city all alone. I'd moved
when I was a newlywed, so I never had to navigate the concrete jungle
on my own. Maybe I *could* be of some benefit to this young woman.

The training session was pretty straightforward. It reinforced the
most basic yet essential skills we can implement when we are mentoring.
First, listen. Then listen some more. Ask questions. Then ask more questions. Engage in your mentee's life and ask about issues. Ask the hard
questions when necessary. And don't just offer advice. Try to talk through
problems and work together for a strategy or resolution. (I know what
you're thinking. This is great advice for any relationship, isn't it?)

To make a long story short, Keeley and I started meeting, and as
Amira had predicted, we got along splendidly. And four years later, we
still meet. Keeley has become a dear friend, and I greatly value our
conversations. I talked with her when she first began dating the man
who would become her husband. We discuss how to navigate the cut-
throat New York City world of modeling and acting. And we share
the trials and triumphs of her life as a newlywed. She helps me just as
much as I try to help her. Not every setup will result in this kind of relationship, but good can still result. Speaking from experience and

being glad I was willing to take a risk, I encourage you—when a mentor opportunity presents itself—to give it a try!

Takeaway:

1. Are you wondering where you might find a mentor—or a mentee? Try these possibilities:

   + At work

   + At church

   + In your neighborhood

   + In your social circle

   + In your volunteer activities

   + Via professional mentor arrangements

2. Be open to meeting people and getting to know them. Be flexible and willing to try a unique game plan, be it casual or formal.

3. Who are your current mentors? Whom would you like to have mentor you—and what are you going to do to see if that can happen? If you're not in a mentoring relationship as a mentor or a mentee, take a risk and develop one. By blessing others, your own life will be doubly blessed.

Treat people as if they are what they ought to be,
and you can help them become what they are capable of becoming.
—JOHANN VON GOETHE

*D*o you believe you can change the world? Hugh O'Brian, the famous actor and philanthropist, believes an individual can change the world, no matter their age, ethnicity, faith, or economic status. He brought those values to life when he founded Hugh O'Brian Youth Leadership in 1958. HOBY's mission is to inspire and develop our global community of volunteers and alumni to a lifetime dedicated to leadership, service, and innovation. Each year more than 12,000 students participate in the HOBY youth leadership program, joining the more than 450,000 alumni who have done the same over fifty-eight years.

Consider the example of Marta Belcher, who attended HOBY in 2012. Inspired by HOBY to develop a long-term vision yet make an immediate impact, she became executive director of No Worries Now, a nonprofit dedicated to improving the lives of teens who have life-threatening illnesses. Realizing that umbilical cord blood can cure leukemia and other cancers that many No Worries Now patients are battling, Marta developed public cord-blood banking legislation efforts at the state and national levels. All lawmakers needed was a bit of encouragement to get going.

Megan was a HOBY ambassador from Washington State in 1996, and she used her HOBY experience as a stepping-stone into her future career. We hope all young people reading this book will be inspired to take the leap of faith in their lives, whatever goals or dreams they have. Megan is a reminder that anyone, anytime, and anywhere can make a difference. Hugh and I love this chapter and hope it will inspire others to run to launching-pad programs all around them and jump for the stars! *You* can change the world.

—Javier La Fianza, CEO of HOBY,
and Hugh O'Brian, actor and founder

Five

Launching Pads

Finding Experiences in Life That Can Give You a Boost!

*Small opportunities are often
the beginning of great achievements.*

—UNKNOWN

REMEMBER THOSE MOMENTS when a space shuttle would take off into the sky? The energy, the power, the burst of smoke and steam that billowed from the engine and shot the rocket into the atmosphere made the launch an amazing sight. And it often seemed like the whole world stopped for a moment and focused its attention on that liftoff. It took tremendous effort to get that shuttle off the ground, but the result was always spectacular. The shuttle zoomed into the sky and headed for the unknown frontier beyond Earth. But what made this all possible? The launchpad. The rocket needed all that power behind it to get it going in the first place. A starting point; a place to get that huge boost of energy; a beginning!

Perhaps you are feeling like opportunities never come your way. Maybe you are getting frustrated as you look around for your first job, or discouraged with where you are in your career right now. You can't seem to get your engine going. Here's a secret: Launching Pads don't always come to us, sometimes we need to go to them. And we need to be looking for them.

I recently gave the keynote address at Penn State for the Powerful Women Paving the Way business conference. After my speech, I got a familiar question from my audience. "How do I launch my career? How do I get going?" This is the most common question I get.

Start by assessing the world around you. What launching pad activities are available to you at school? In college? At work or in your neighborhood? Make a careful evaluation of any opportunities that might help launch you toward your career goal. I do believe there is no such thing as luck in our careers. Luck defined is "when preparation meets opportunity." Let me share a few stories about how I found my launching pads.

My Launching Pads

Two programs stand out to me as starting points.

The first I've already mentioned: the pageant called National American Miss. I certainly didn't grow up a pageant girl or, frankly, ever have any thoughts of participating in a pageant. But for some reason when that flyer came in the mail one day, my mom mentioned it seemed like a fun idea, and I jumped on it. I'm forever grateful I did. I describe National American Miss as a corporate team-building retreat wrapped up in a kids' summer camp teaching real-life skills. What made this a launching pad for me wasn't the fact that it was a pageant; the pageant served as a launching pad because of the experiences involved in the competition. I learned to present myself well, to walk out in front of a large audience, to speak in a microphone clearly and confidently, and to sit down and interview well with an adult. These foundational skills, which aren't always taught to tweens or teens, have served me well in my career and in life in general.

If you are a younger reader or if you have daughters who are eighteen years old or younger, National American Miss (NAM) is just a cool program. This nationwide organization is run by some wonderful people. And as wild as it may sound, NAM is a great place for networking. I still keep in touch with many women I met through their pageants. Several were bridesmaids in my wedding! I still reach out to girls in the network on a regular basis, and I produce and host NAM events with my husband. NAM taught me to be brave, to put myself out there, and to start building the best me at an early age. Now when the camera's red light comes on and I go live as a TV reporter, I often remember the first time I held the microphone and walked onstage as a twelve-year-old at my NAM pageant. The same adrenaline and excitement still pulse through my veins.

You never know where a particular launching pad may take you. As I mentioned, I now have the privilege each summer of helping to produce and host some of the NAM events across the country. I find a great deal of satisfaction in "paying it forward" to the generations following me while I get to spend time talking with and mentoring these young girls with big dreams. I'm reminded constantly of the importance of programs like this one when the parents stop me in the hallways to tell me stories of their daughters' journeys. By putting themselves out there into an environment like NAM, these young ladies are building skills that will benefit them for their entire lives.

The second influential program that served as a launching pad for me was the Hugh O'Brian Youth Leadership organization (HOBY) for high school sophomores. Administrators choose student leaders from across America to write essays about what leadership means to them. A boy and a girl from each participating high school are chosen as ambassadors and attend a four-day HOBY retreat in their states. There, these sophomores participate in dozens of breakout sessions, lectures, games, projects, and—again—networking opportunities. I left my HOBY retreat with a totally different worldview—I better understood how to fight peer pressure, engage my peers, and set goals for my academic future.

For over five decades HOBY has inspired young people to become catalysts for positive change in their home, school, workplace, and community. HOBY's founder, actor Hugh O'Brian, started the program after he took a life-changing trip to Africa to meet the famed humanitarian Dr. Albert Schweitzer. HOBY now boasts more than 425,000 alumni and is growing. I have also had the privilege of hosting the New York leadership awards for HOBY at the Plaza Hotel in New York City. I love seeing these students experience what I did so many years ago. And I continue to both network with my fellow HOBY alumni and apply the leadership and problem-solving skills I learned from HOBY to my current job.

I learned valuable life lessons and skills from both these programs that I still use today:

✦ Defining who I am: National American Miss asked me to put together a résumé and explain my ambitions for life. So, at the age of twelve, I was asking myself, *What do I want to be when I grow up—and why? What can I do to earn good grades in school? What will I do to serve in my community?* HOBY asked me to develop a business plan and encouraged me to try to get into the best college possible. It was great to be involved in programs that challenged me to know myself better, to be the best I could be, and to set goals and aim high.

✦ Networking: At NAM, I met like-minded twelve-year-old girls all going through the rough times of junior high. I gained a bigger picture of life when I thought about future career possibilities. I was surrounded by positive peer pressure to be and do more than I imagined. At HOBY, I met high-achieving high school sophomores from all over the state, from all walks of life, and from all backgrounds. We all strived for a better life, and we wanted to help change the world. This energy and enthusiasm were contagious!

✦ Providing support for the future and an alumni network: National American Miss recruits many former pageants girls to work as staff, providing great summer jobs for college students and continued networking. The HOBY network is vast and holds alumni events all over the country, so opportunities aren't limited to one demographic and there's no limit to the amount of years to participate. As mentioned, I still host the HOBY NY Albert Schweitzer leadership awards banquet every year.

✦ Paying it forward: Just as a sorority has Big Sisters and Little Sisters, these programs encourage older members to mentor and encourage the younger members. Everyone benefits from an organization that promotes this kind of camaraderie and fellowship.

NAM and HOBY were helpful organizations for me, and many others—Girl Scouts, Girls Inc., Junior Achievement, YMCA sports, Decca for debate, performing arts summer camps—are out there. Programs like these make excellent launching pads, and many offer scholarships for those who can't afford them, so don't be afraid to ask.

One of my favorite questions to ask when I interview a celebrity is this: "At what moment in your young life did you realize you wanted to pursue this career full-time?" Almost every successful person in entertainment, media, or journalism—and business, education, medicine, or law as well—had unique launching pads.

Stay Alert!

Opportunities are like sunrises: if you wait too long, you miss them.
—WILLIAM ARTHUR WARD

Sometimes these opportunities will pop up suddenly and with little notice. We must be on the lookout for them. My friend Regina Moore, who is now the top casting director in the Southeast, shared with me this story about her college days when she was pursuing film. Regina and her friends heard that *The Last of the Mohicans* was filming in North Carolina and looking for extras. The set was a fifteen-hour drive from her home, but she felt this was a once-in-a-lifetime experience she needed to pursue. When would a major motion picture be filming any closer? Chances were slim!

So she convinced some friends they needed to go. They packed up the car and headed to North Carolina. Fifteen hours later, the minute they pulled up to the site, she knew she had made the right decision. To be on a movie set and see all the moving parts—the wardrobe and makeup, the crew setting up the cameras, the cast practicing their lines, the hustle and bustle of all the bodies on set, the director calling action, catching a glimpse of the lead actor Daniel Day-Lewis—was a priceless experience. This was a launching-pad moment for Regina. As she drove home, she decided she wanted to work in the film industry. Recognizing how much she loved the process of putting together a film, she knew she wanted to work in casting.

I often wonder how she heard about that filming. Was it a flyer someone posted in her dorm? Did a drama teacher make a quick announcement at the end of class? Or maybe a friend just casually mentioned it? In any case, it's important to be alert for those opportunities Sometimes they come unexpectedly and will need to be acted on quickly. We always need to make the effort and take the time to discern if they are right for us.

Opportunities May Require You to Take a Leap of Faith . . . and Have Lots of Energy!

> *Make the most of each day, whatever turns up, grab it and do it and heartily! This is your time, for life is short.*
> —ECCLESIASTES 9:7-10

Now, I don't want to make it sound as if launching pads only happen early in your career. They keep happening! One recent launching-pad moment for me came in January 2016. A friend of mine, Brian Williams, had been named CEO of a company called Dance Network. Brian and I had connected through mutual friends in LA, and he knew I wanted to be more involved with film, either acting or producing. Over coffee, he casually mentioned a dance movie called *Heartbeats* that was about to begin filming in Mumbai, India. Duane Adler had written the script and signed on to direct the film. (Duane is famous for writing the screenplays for the movies *Step Up* and *Save the Last Dance*.) Brian knew that Duane was looking for someone to play the part of judge and host in the final scene. Brian casually asked if I might be interested in the part and willing to fly to India for four days for the shoot. I remember thinking, *Well, that could really be fun, but fly to Mumbai? I have a five-month-old baby . . . probably not.* Even though he knew I was hesitant because of my baby, he told me he would like to give my name to Duane anyway. I said, "Sure. Why not?" I left thinking I would never again hear about the film project.

A week later, though, I learned that the film's producers had received my résumé and headshot and were interested in casting me. But they needed me to fly to Mumbai in less than two weeks, and I needed to have a business visa to do so. I gulped when I read that text. *A business visa? To India?* I have traveled all over the world, but never to India. I'd had a few small parts in movies, but none that required me to fly halfway across the world on extremely short notice. I immediately headed to my computer and googled "get business visa to work in Mumbai, India, quickly."

Seizing the Opportunity Wasn't Easy

The Consulate General of India in New York City popped up. I called one number . . . was transferred to another number . . . and ended up with a very nice person who told me that it takes two to three weeks, minimum, to get a visa, therefore meeting the producer's schedule was highly unlikely. I was welcome to apply, but I would need to do so in person at the Indian embassy in New York. And as for the paperwork that needed to be filled out? Let's put it this way: You know how frustrating it is to get a driver's license renewed at the DMV? Getting a business visa was double that trouble!

I called my husband and asked him what he thought. We figured it would be four days of filming, but I would be gone six days, because it takes a full day of flying to get there and another full day getting back. My husband gave his typical enthusiastic answer: "Keep pursuing this. It probably won't work, but at least you tried. It's India! You have to try!" I agreed. Besides, both of us were convinced the embassy would never get me the business visa in time and that would settle that.

But when the producers made me a formal offer, I got to work on getting that visa. They told me I had to make it to India by a certain day to film my role, or it would not work out. I had four working days to pull this off. I gathered all my documents and headed to the Indian embassy right after work at *Inside Edition* on Tuesday. Although the embassy was close to the studio, I got there just as it was closing. I totally had one of those scenes from a movie where the guard—standing on the inside—was about to lock the door, and I held up my hand and said, "Hey! Wait a minute, please! May I talk to you?" The guard begrudgingly opened the door. I told him earnestly about my trip and that I needed to apply for a visa and had all my papers. He looked at me and said, "Come back tomorrow morning. We're closed now." And he shut the door.

I returned the next morning a full half hour before the embassy opened, and at least ten people were already in line. About two hours later, when I finally turned in all my papers, I told the person helping me that, in order to make my trip, I needed my visa on Monday. She looked at me as if I had asked for the moon. She said, "That is highly unlikely because Friday is New Year's Eve, and we are working a half day, and the applications won't even get processed till tomorrow afternoon. Most of the time this process takes at least two or three weeks. You can track your visa application online. Good luck." And that was it! She took my passport, and I watched her toss it onto a pile of other applications for visas. Now I couldn't even fly to India as a tourist because they had my passport! (Don't think I hadn't thought about doing that.)

The next day I logged in to track my application. In the morning I saw absolutely no progress. I was pretty convinced this trip to India wouldn't happen. When the movie folks asked what my status was, I told them I would know first thing Monday morning: I would either be on a plane to India . . . or not. They asked me to keep them posted.

That night, when I logged back on—and to my utter amazement—my status read "Application received and being processed." This was Thursday night. The next day was New Year's Eve, and the offices were closing at noon. In the morning, when I logged on, my status read "Application processed." That weekend I just kept praying and asking God to let "His will be done."

But I wasn't in the clear yet, so I didn't let myself get too excited. I still needed to fly back to New York City, show up at the Embassy of India on Monday morning, wait in line, and ask for my business visa to be retrieved from the stack of recently processed applications. So that weekend I just kept praying and asking God to let His will be done. I flew back to New York City on Sunday night and was at the embassy door a full hour and a half before it opened. No one was going to beat me to that first-in-line position!

I stood there at the entrance at 7:30 a.m., in the freezing cold, with my teeth chattering and my fingers frozen. The doors opened and I walked to the counter, where I learned that picking up visas was always done in the afternoon and I would need to come back. I explained that my flight was leaving this evening and I needed to put in a full day's work at *Inside Edition* before I got on that plane. I needed to get my visa now! The person at the help desk told me to have a seat. They gave me no guarantees they would find my visa in time. They were going to process all the passport and tourist visa requests first. I sat next to a nice man who told me he had heard stories about people waiting four hours for their visas. I smiled and silently prayed that would not be me.

About thirty minutes later the help desk called out my name. They had my business visa! I thanked everyone profusely, dashed out the door, jumped into a cab, and emailed the producers in Mumbai, telling them I was on my way. I got on my plane that night, and fif-teen hours later I landed in Mumbai. I soon heard director Duane Adler calling, "Action!" What a fantastic experience it was. And I almost didn't make it.

Energy, Persistence, and Value

At numerous points I could have decided the visa process was too hard: *I don't have time to collect my driver's license, my birth certificate, my marriage license—and get a passport photo,* or *I don't want to fly back to New York City and stand in line in the freezing cold at 7:00 a.m. outside that embassy,* or even *I don't want to be on a plane for fifteen hours, only to land in a country where I know no one and don't know the language, and be away from my family and newborn son for six days.*

But I am *so glad I did.* This film was a launching pad for me in so many ways. First, I got to meet the cast and crew and develop some incredible contacts. Then, I was directed by Duane Adler! To be on set with him, to watch him guide the entire cast and crew—I was seeing pure magic happen. I was learning from a master. Our main cinematographer, Ravi Varman, was always available to talk, and he told me stories about working with Christian Bale on *Batman* and Martin Scorsese on his films. He offered insight and information about the film industry that I will carry with me forever. Actor Justin Chon, who played one of my fellow judges and had appeared in the *Twilight* movies, had very interesting ideas about acting classes and how to develop a character.

The experience was incredible for me personally and professionally. It has served as a launching pad into other acting endeavors. The contacts I made, the doors to business opportunities that may open in the future, and the chance to have an all-expenses-paid trip to the beautiful country of India are invaluable. In fact, I ended up believing so much in the film and the people involved that I took the leap of faith to become a producer. So in addition to having a small acting role, I also joined the business side of the project and am continuing to learn more about the industry. One more reason standing in line at the embassy was so worth it.

Whenever launching pads occur, they may require energy and persistence, but they are so worth it.

> *Nothing is more expensive than a missed opportunity.*
> —H. JACKSON BROWN, JR.

Opportunities Missed?

My husband attended the University of Houston and majored in marketing. He took some fascinating business classes, one of which was taught by a former executive for the Mars Candy Company (think M&Ms, Snickers, Milky Way, Twix). It was in that class that a launching pad passed him by.

Every year the professor of one of his marketing classes ran a sales competition for his students and would take the winner out to lunch in his Porsche. In addition to going to school, my husband was working full-time to help launch a startup company. So, because he was "too busy" getting his degree and working, he passed on the opportunity to participate. He looks back now and regrets that decision. What a unique and interesting opportunity, to sit down with a former high-ranking executive with a major worldwide brand! Not only would that experience have been cool then, but years later what a wonderful contact and mentor my husband might have had. Likewise, there were similar programs at my college that I also did not pursue and now regret. Don't let those moments pass you by.

Be the Launching Pad

And if you are well along in your career, you may be at a point where you can offer someone a launching pad. Don't think you need a lot of money or resources to do it. I don't have a lot of extra time or money right now. My kids are young; I travel a ton for work; and I cover a lot of our family expenses. But a few years ago I found a way to offer a launching pad to others. Every year at my high school, I offer as an auction item the chance to shadow me at *Inside Edition* for a day. One student flies to New York City and sees what it takes to be a national TV news reporter. The student sits next to me at my desk, meets and chats with my colleagues, goes on a story with me, helps carry the equipment, watches me edit the story, and then sees the final product. Then we go out to dinner and talk about what we saw as well as what it means to be a Christian in a secular industry.

I realize we all have different situations, surroundings, income levels, support systems, and skill sets. But sometimes all we have to do is take a brief timeout and look around us to see what opportunities are within reach.

Consider the fact that colleges report scholarship money left unclaimed each year. Isn't that incredible? Similarly, when I applied to be the HOBY ambassador for my high school, I was told that two people had applied. Only two! I could not believe more people didn't seek out this incredible opportunity. Fewer people than we might think are competing for these opportunities. So go for it! Seek out launching pads and see where they take you.

Takeaway:

1. Opportunities won't come to you, sometimes you must go to them.

2. Take advantage of opportunities and use them as stepping-stones.

3. Be alert—they may appear quickly and quietly.

4. When possible and able, offer launching pad opportunities to others.

*M*y husband and I are the international directors of Models for Christ/gModa, a nonprofit ministry that supports fashion professionals around the world. We have modeled for *Cosmopolitan*, Hugo Boss, Hermès, and more. We have seen it all. In our industry, there are many stories of people who have had to make choices under highly stressful situations regarding what they will or will not do as models. We, and others, have learned to take a stand and sometimes explain to our agents why we need to turn down a job paying thousands of dollars because it conflicts with our beliefs. Sometimes it works out, and sometimes it does not. However, there are also many good jobs in the modeling world that portray life and hope and are well within our personal standards.

Our dear friend Megan furthers this conversation with her own stories from the red carpet and how, as a believer, she has navigated the pressure to deliver for her job while also upholding her personal morals. No matter what job we have, we have to make many choices in life and at work, and these choices often significantly impact us and those around us.

Above all, for us in the fashion world and beyond, it is important to remember that these are our bodies, our images, and our lives, and although Jesus offers freedom and forgives us for our mistakes, these choices result in images that do not go away and there are often consequences that remain. Choose wisely.

—Christina and Shane Nearman, Models for Christ/gModa

Six

Red Carpet Realities

The Business of the Red Carpet

> *Seek to be worth knowing rather than well known.*
> —SANDRA TURLEY

*Y*ES, IT CAN BE SURREAL. I'm talking about one of the seemingly more glamorous parts of my job: interviewing and interacting with celebrities on the red carpet. Yes, it's pretty wild to watch a movie or TV show and the next day see the stars walk into the *Inside Edition* studios or up to me on the red carpet for an interview.

I work in this magical and bizarre world where the people I see on the front page of the newspaper, in the top story on television news programs, or in the latest blockbuster will probably be a person I interview in a matter of days. My fellow reporter, Les Trent, and I often pick up the *New York Post* or *People* magazine, point to the picture on the cover, and say, "I wonder which one of us will be hanging out with this person next week!"

What you see on television are a few minutes from my interactions and interviews with the different celebrities in what looks like me having a long conversation with a friend. But you may be surprised to learn that these interviews do not create friendships or even relationships. People assume these celebrities are my friends and that our interactions occur much more often than they really do.

The fact is, most of my relationships with celebrities and politicians are incredibly one-sided. I ask all the questions, and they give all the answers. So I end up knowing everything about them, and they know very little about me. Having done this for enough years now and seeing the same faces on the countless red carpets, yes, many of the celebrities have gotten to know me, but our interactions are for one reason: to promote themselves and a project or product so *Inside Edition*'s six million nightly viewers will learn all about it. Our time is limited and we are both on the red carpet for a purpose.

Occasionally there are a few instances where circumstances have allowed for a longer and more in-depth interaction. The Super Bowl has provided for this. Our show has hired several celebrity guest correspondents to work with me for the entire week leading up to the Super Bowl. Therefore, I got several days to get to know and interact with Gabby Douglas, Shawn Johnson, and Katherine Webb. All three of these ladies became friends of mine. All three of these women are well-known celebrities in their own right, but this time their job was to join me—so to speak—on the other side of the red carpet for a week. Anytime we step into someone else's shoes or step out of our comfort zones, we appreciate one another more, and this has been the case with these ladies. In some instances I have built friendships with the people I've had lengthier interviews with. But, for the most part, conversations on the red carpet are quite short, one-sided, and completely about the celebrity.

Brand-new celebrities often have a hard time with this. When Carrie Underwood first started winning country music awards after winning *American Idol*, I would ask about her dress when we talked on the red carpet. Instead of waiting for my next question, like the usual celebrity on the red carpet would, she would ask me about my dress and jewelry! She is a naturally kind and friendly person. I'm sure her publicist eventually told her, "Carrie, they want to know about you! Just answer the question and let the interviewer continue."

You see this skill exemplified in pros like Nicole Kidman or Angelina Jolie. They instantly respond to my question and then smile as they wait for the next one. Then they sort of dismiss me with a smile or a thank-you and walk to the next interviewer. For them, this is simply their job. It's almost like a business transaction: the celebrities offer a service they know is valuable.

Such celebrities seem so confident walking that red carpet, but we often hear that celebrities are actually insecure people. I think I know one of the reasons that might be the case: some of them forget how to have normal relationships. Publicizing themselves and their work must be difficult to turn off. There are definitely exceptions to the rule. The majority of the country music stars I interview, for example, stay pretty down to earth and friendly. The Hollywood actors and actresses appear to be more guarded. And I think it is because in Hollywood, they understand there is fierce competition to promote themselves and their projects to the media. If you don't understand this aspect of the red carpet, it can seem very narcissistic.

Still, I am thankful for the experience of the red carpet because it provides a very interesting look at society and at a unique form of human interaction. I've come to a place where I can treat the red carpet as work, yet enjoy it and appreciate why it is a necessary and exciting part of our industry. But I recognize it is not meant to be more than that. It is a business, and the majority of those interactions and interviews will be temporary and professional. In other words, the red carpet isn't a place for deep friendships.

In fact, and probably not surprisingly, those interviews on the red carpet cause me to desire deep and genuine relationships in my life. I also think working on the red carpet has changed me from an extrovert into something of an introvert. Now instead of enjoying being in a loud and busy crowd, I long more and more for times when I can engage with people one-on-one, get to know them better, and am free to share what's going on with me. I want to really see people and have them see me.

So what can we learn from life on the red carpet? Here are a few principles I want to share that may be interesting and helpful to learn.

✦ Remember That Perfection Doesn't Exist

On the red carpet, celebrities have teams of hair, makeup, and clothing experts on hand. They spend countless hours selecting designer outfits and having them tailored to fit their bodies perfectly. The artists sort through dozens of hairstyles to make sure theirs are the most glamorous or flattering. The stars commit thousands of dollars to exfoliating, polishing, tanning, and painting their skin to appear flawless. Their stylists stay nearby at all times to make sure the clothing, the hair, and the makeup look impeccable every second. I have had publicists stop interviews and ask me for a few seconds to powder their clients' noses or fix bobby pins in their hair. And let's not forget, once those photos are taken on the red carpet, they are still often airbrushed or Photoshopped before they go to press.

Of course there's no such thing as perfection. And the appearance of perfection doesn't come without a ton of effort and maintenance. Furthermore, by whose standards do we judge perfection? Society's definition of what is perfect is actually often unhealthy and harmful! (Consider, for example, the level of thinness society declares normal and acceptable. For many people that standard might be dangerous.) I share this behind-the-scenes truth for those women who see photos from the red carpet and compare their bodies, makeup, hair, and wardrobes to those of the celebrities. It's not a fair comparison. I also share these facts for the young girls who think they need to invest hundreds of dollars on high-end makeup, jewelry, hairstyles, or clothing. No matter what you do, you won't be picture-perfect—and that's okay!

Sure, when I do my interviews, I sometimes find myself comparing my legs or hair to the celebrity I am interviewing. It is hard not to! Right after I had my second baby, Catcher, I was assigned to work with Miss Universe, Pia Wurtzbach, during Super Bowl week. Imagine that, standing next to Miss Universe right after having a baby! Sure, I felt insecure. But once I met Pia, I realized she is a human being like everyone else. I got to know her as a friend and really enjoyed my time with her.

I tried to move from comparing myself to her to working alongside her. She had qualities to offer our show I did not, such as a worldwide fan base, and I had the sports knowledge and presentation skills to deliver the news of the Super Bowl to our audience. We made a pretty good pair! But like anyone else, I had to get over that initial gulp of insecurity when I first got the assignment. Pia is incredibly beautiful but, like all of us, she has taken photos for magazines that were airbrushed. She, along with every other celebrity, has bad hair days. Everyone has uneven skin and wrinkles. It's so important we remember this and give ourselves a break.

I see these celebrities on their best days after they receive the best of professional attention. Even J.Lo and Carrie roll out of bed with messy hair, and they wear sweatpants just like the rest of us. I handle my insecurities by remembering what the Bible says: I am "fearfully and wonderfully made" (Psalm 139:14 NIV), and "people look at the outward appearance, but the LORD looks at the heart" (1 Samuel 16:7 NIV). God does desire that we strive to be the best we can be, to take care of our bodies, and to glorify Him with our talents, but His love for us does not at all depend on our physical appearance or our performance. The next time you are comparing yourself to a magazine cover or photo, remember that image is part of a *business*—the business of looking good. That person on the cover is a human being just like you, and they have bad hair days just like you!

✦ Be God's Light

I interview people on the red carpet as part of my job, and I want to turn in excellent work. I don't do those interviews to make friends, yet I don't need to disappear altogether. I can still maintain who I am; I can still be God's best version of myself. To be specific, I can be friendly and treat people with unwavering respect. I can make these business transactions as personable and authentic as possible. If you are genuine and strive to treat everyone with dignity, you will bring God glory.

Sometimes I need to remind myself that the celebrities, crew, production team, and I are all meeting to make a sort of exchange: the celebrities want to deliver a message, whether about a new movie, a fashion line, or certain hot topics. It's my job to ask the questions that will get the most meaningful answers and then deliver the details to our audience. My crew is there to capture the video from the best angles with good lighting and to make sure all the audio levels sound great on your television. It is a team effort, with lots of bells and whistles. It is a business. And sometimes we have a job in that business. Whatever I'm doing, I need to perform it to the best of my ability. The apostle Paul said it this way: "Whatever you do, do your work heartily, as to the Lord rather than for men" (Colossians 3:23). God wants us to do superior work, whether we are on a red carpet or in a courtroom, kitchen, or classroom. You and I are in those places for good reasons and we should do our jobs with excellence.

✦ Mind Those Minutes

You know, those two-minute red carpet interviews I've done have taught me the value of time. They have helped me realize that every increment of time is priceless, so I'd better be prepared. My high school acting coach used to say, "Every day is an audition." And this is true in every profession. Careers can be made or derailed in just a minute or two. This goes for red carpet reporters, too! On the rare occasion when I have been able to bring a friend to the red carpet to observe my work, the most common response I get is, "Wow, I had no idea how hectic and fast-paced a red carpet is!" One particular story summarizes this well. Miley Cyrus was hosting the CMT Music awards with her father, Billy Ray, a few years back, and she had a horrible case of strep throat. Her father was walking down the red carpet and everyone wanted to ask him questions. He walked quickly by me and I had about five seconds to ask him how Miley was feeling. He looked at me and gave me a nice long answer. That answer ended up being the lead story in our show that night! If I hadn't been paying attention and had missed Billy Ray walking down the carpet, I would have lost that whole story, and in turn, let my boss down.

So watch those minutes and hours! Stay alert on the job. Don't waste a single one. As 1 Corinthians 15:58 says, "Be steadfast, immovable, always abounding in the work of the Lord, knowing that your toil is not *in vain* in the Lord."

✦ If You Want Good Results, Put In Good Effort

Nothing worth doing is ever easy. In my line of work, the mechanics and setup of the red carpet can be very stressful. Yes, celebrities are smiling and wearing beautiful gowns and classy tuxes. On TV the event looks like an effortless and delightful party. But in reality the media are monitoring thousands of details in order to deliver these images of easy elegance to the public. Days of hard work have gone into preparing for this three- or four-hour event. Just as a physician studies for years to spend a few hours a day operating on a patient or a lawyer puts in long hours of research and study to give his relatively brief closing argument in court, so we the media prepare for the red carpet in innumerable ways during what I call our surgery hours.

Key to our preparation is reading publications like *People*, *USA Today*, and countless websites and trade magazines. We receive weekly, if not daily, press releases from publicists and managers filling us in on their clients' careers. And we monitor all the celebrities' social media. In fact, when someone works in entertainment television, tracking social media is a regular part of the workday. Just as my father, who is a financial analyst, reads the *Financial Times* and checks the stock market throughout the day, so we in the entertainment industry are continually reading entertainment news.

Once the nominees and presenters for a specific awards show are announced, we can do some final studying of specific people. But always being up to speed on entertainment news in general is, I think, the best preparation. Quite frequently a surprise guest—someone not scheduled to appear—will walk the red carpet at an awards show, and if you are a news junkie, you will know who that person is and what to ask.

Nashville's annual Country Music Association Awards is a good example of a red carpet event. The industry's biggest night of the year, the Country Music Awards show starts for the media at about 4:00 p.m. and lasts until the awards show begins, which is usually 7:00 p.m. Between 5:00 and 6:00— the hour I actually spend on the red carpet—the celebrities arrive, and the pace is fast! As a reporter, I have to stay alert and sharp. If I stumble through a greeting or blank out on a question, I risk losing a celebrity's attention or having a publicist jump in and pull his or her client away from me. Then I've lost an opportunity to ask an important question or, worse, missed a celebrity who was waiting in the wings. That person could move on and skip me completely because they've seen me fumbling my interviews. And if I'm distracted by my mistakes, I might even miss the big-name celebrities who have to be called over.

Positions on the red carpet are hugely important and highly regulated. It is not first come, first served, and there is a pecking order. Each media outlet is assigned their position usually based on how popular your show is. *Inside Edition*, which gets around six million viewers a night, tends to get a high position on the red carpet, but not as high as some of our competition because we don't just do entertainment.

Someone like Taylor Swift or Faith Hill, for example, will take only one or two questions from the media who are in the very first positions. Once Faith or Taylor talks to this outlet, she will walk quickly down the red carpet, smile at other reporters, but probably not be planning to give any more interviews. It is my job, then, to try to call her over and have a short chat with her.

Clearly, I need to multitask. I need to pay attention to the celebrity standing in front of me and giving me an interview while I look out of the corner of my eye and see which big celebrities are walking by. I need to find a way to catch the eye of that artist or her publicist, politely wrap up the interview I am conducting, and then launch into another intriguing interview—all in a matter of seconds.

Every profession has something similar to this especially intense hour on the red carpet. In sports, it might be the fourth quarter. In a play or musical, it might be the second act. For a college student, it might be a final exam, and for a race car driver, it might be the last lap. For a stay-at-home mom or dad, it might be the breakfast hour before school or the witching hour of doing homework and fixing dinner. During this hour, we need to concentrate, buckle down, focus, and deliver. We can't get too frazzled. We need to keep our cool . . . and hustle!

✦ Think Ahead

The fast-paced, 24/7 world of constant news makes it imperative that journalists consider how to *advance the story*, and Charles Lachman, my boss at *Inside Edition*, is a genius at this. He looks not only at today's story but at tomorrow's potential stories and the possibilities for the day after that, for next week, and for next month. This skill takes a while to learn, hone, and master. I worked at *Inside Edition* for a few years before I got the hang of it. But I have learned to anticipate stories that might arise, so I'll be ready for them.

One time this played out for me (no pun intended) was Super Bowl 49 when the Seahawks faced the Patriots. On the Tuesday before the big Sunday game, I covered Seahawks cornerback Richard Sherman chatting with the media for a few minutes. I had learned a few days prior that his girlfriend was nine months pregnant. My boss hadn't asked me to interview Sherman about this, nor was the press really covering the story yet. But I had a feeling it would be big news: she could go into labor at any moment and pull this valuable defender from the game, or Sunday would come around and suddenly people might spot this very pregnant woman at the game and start talking about it. So I asked Richard Sherman some sports questions, and then I asked about his pregnant girlfriend: What was his game plan? If she went into labor, would he leave the game? I saved this tape and continued about my business.

Sure enough, the Friday before the Super Bowl, the media started buzzing about this story. But by Friday Richard Sherman and the rest of the Super Bowl players were no longer giving interviews. Because I had asked him about his girlfriend earlier in the week, *Inside Edition* was able to run a full story on this topic and use my interview. My boss was pleased, and I was proud of myself for thinking ahead.

Whew! (But It's Fun, Too!)

Despite my emphasis on how hard I work and the intensity of certain aspects of the job, don't get me wrong! I love my work. The red carpet can be very enjoyable, and I've gleaned quite a few life lessons from my favorite interviews.

One topic that is good for such insights is what these celebrities believe is the key to their success. Dolly Parton believes you need to surround yourself with smart and positive people; Donald Trump says you must be confident and discerning, and have a great education; and Oprah shares that you must listen to what your soul says. I have had the opportunity to sing with Darius Rucker, chat with Gisele Bündchen about her family right after her husband, Tom Brady, led the Patriots to Super Bowl victory, and talk about teen issues of the day with the casts of *Gossip Girl* and the newly rebooted *90210*. All these celebrities offered some insight into the keys to their success.

Does this sound exhilarating but exhausting? It is definitely both! Once the red carpet coverage is complete, do I want to attend parties and keep the fun going all night long? No way! I want to go home, put on my pj's, and crawl into bed. Or I want to go find some friends, kick off my shoes, and order a pizza. Sometimes I can do this—choose between sleep and celebrating—but not always, because I am a wife and a mother of two.

My husband is great, though. He has learned how stressful the red carpet can be, so he usually puts the kids to bed on those nights and understands I may need an hour or two to unwind when I get home. We have learned how important it is to adequately detox and relax, even for just a few minutes. When I don't take that time, there are consequences. I have been cranky and yelled at my family when I didn't take the time to detox. I have missed friends' birthdays and worn my body out and gotten sick. Winding down is important!

I think it's crucial to remember that organization and preparation are important before, during, and after an event. It's an ongoing process.

For me, it's remembering that working the red carpet is much more than meets the eye, and I have to be mindful of the entire process, not just the day of the event.

Covering the red carpet is a necessary aspect of my work, and the glamour is fun, but it is important to remember that it's a business event, not real life. The celebrities and media are not engaging in regular, healthy relationships on the red carpet; what happens there is more of a transaction intended to advance a career or advertise a movie or TV series. If I don't understand and remember this, the red carpet can be dangerous to my self-esteem (I can't measure up to the unrealistic standards set by those celebrities); communication skills (I may become self-focused and miss seeing other people's needs); and behavior (I may begin to think the world revolves around me). God created us to be social beings who need authentic, real relationships—not the glitzy, breezy ones we see onscreen. So we—and this is true whatever our line of work—should make sure our lives are supplemented with healthy relationships with people at church, school, and other activities.

Takeaway:

1. What's business is business. The red carpet is a business. Remember to keep a proper perspective between business and personal.

2. The red carpet is not reality. Celebrities have full teams help them look so effortlessly flawless! Do not compare or place unrealistic expectations on yourself.

3. Staying grounded is important. We can do this through our faith, family, and friends.

*T*he entertainment business and values don't always go hand in hand. It's often a struggle to keep from falling into the traps of the business. I'd love to say my integrity and core values have always fueled my career and guided my life path. And for the most part, they have.

Looking back, I have as much pride in my mistakes as I do my successes. They're both mine. I realize they both make me the person I am today. A person who is better than he was yesterday and not as good as he can be tomorrow. It's not a perfect line to that goal. There are dips. There are struggles. But each day I begin with a promise to myself to try and get as close to that goal as possible—to treat all people fairly, equally, and with the respect they deserve, to stay grounded and humble in the glow of success, and to hold my head high in the face of failure.

I've learned to pay attention to three engines in my life: God, family, and a sense of wonder, that curiosity and drive to have new experiences and discover what's around the next corner. God points the way, family is always looking over my shoulder, and my sense of wonder is the chaotic force the other two engines have to keep in check. When all three are firing, my life is bliss. One goes out, though? Hang on! It's going to be a wild ride! And so has been my life. I wouldn't trade it for the world.

—Storme Warren, host, SiriusXM's *The Highway*

Seven

Stepping Out
of the Boat

Why Being a Free Agent Allowed Me
to Play Ball in the Big Leagues

*You gain strength, courage and confidence by every experience
in which you really stop to look fear in the face.*

—ELEANOR ROOSEVELT

*W*ORKING IN MEDIA AND ENTERTAINMENT certainly requires the willingness to take risks. My industry is very fickle. Because entertainment media deals with pop culture, someone can be the toast of the town one day and yesterday's news the next. The competition is fierce. Someone is always looking to take your job or steal your spotlight.

One way to survive and stay relevant is to continue to be very good at what you do but also to diversify your talents and engagements. This used to be frowned upon and the person considered a jack-of-all-trades, master of none. But that's not what I mean here. Diversifying your talents means that in addition to your home-base job, you have your hand in a variety of other endeavors not only to challenge yourself creatively but to provide alternative employment and perhaps greater financial security.

Still Dreaming

I had been with *Inside Edition* as a full-time reporter for four years. Things were going well, and I was working hard to deliver for my boss. But I began to notice that some of my fellow entertainment reporters were doing more than just their day jobs. They had taken on new projects in addition to reporting. For example, Nancy Odell, host of *Entertainment Tonight*, has an eye for interior design and loves home decorating. She parlayed this into a business venture and has launched a furniture line. Maria Menounos, in addition to being an anchor for *E! Entertainment*, had a popular Sirius radio show and created the AfterBuzz TV online media network. She turned her love of gabbing with friends on television into profitable web shows.

I had always known that I wanted to do something in addition to my work at *Inside Edition*. Something that would challenge me, raise my profile, and enhance my personal life. I knew I wanted to leverage my talents and work in many areas of the entertainment industry, the way Nancy and Maria were. And, most important, I wanted to shine my light for Christ.

When I started sharing this desire with other people, they would ask about my interests and what I hoped to accomplish. With those questions as prompts, I began making lists of my dreams. (I had set goals like that when I was in college.) I also set up meetings with different influencers in my industry.

One such meeting was at William Morris Endeavor Entertainment (WME) in New York City. WME is one of the top talent and literary agencies in the world, and how I even got this meeting was interesting. I see now that God had his fingerprints all over it. I had stayed in touch with a childhood friend of mine, Sarah Vicendese—we had played soccer together when we were in grade school—who was working at the public relations firm Sunshine Sachs. She came to

NYC for an event and invited me to join her. We started talking about our career goals and dreams, and I mentioned my desire to branch out and do some complimentary gigs in addition to *Inside Edition*. She recommended I meet with one of her friends at WME. My friend made the introduction, and I made an appointment.

Disappointed But Not Dejected

I remember sitting in the lobby of WME's posh midtown Manhattan offices. Pictures of famous actors, sports stars, and news anchors covered the walls. I was definitely at the big-boy agency. The agent brought me into his office, we sat down, and I started sharing my dreams. He was polite and listened, but soon started challenging me. When I told him I wanted to write a book, he asked me who would buy it and why I felt qualified to write it. When I told him I wanted to pursue acting on the side, he told me the acting world is very competitive, I was basically a nobody, and it would be very tough to get a part in anything. When I told him I was also interested in sports broadcasting, he asked what my experience was. I had no sports broadcasting experience aside from the occasional Super Bowl or NBA finals story I covered for *Inside Edition*. I felt myself getting discouraged.

Then the agent shared several stories about what some of his current clients were doing. He listed, for instance, the executive producers of several of the top national news shows and asked if I had ever met with or sent my tape to any of them. I knew one name, but I had never met her. I didn't know any of the others. The agent told me he didn't really think he could help me, but to keep in touch and send him my demo tape down the road.

I left his office disappointed, but not dejected. He had asked me some really good questions that I didn't know the answers to yet. I needed to narrow my focus, sharpen my skills, get to know the names of the players in my industry—and I needed not to be discouraged that this particular agent didn't want to work with me.

And this, my friends, is the point where I think people tend to give up. I could have walked out of that office and thought, *I can't play in the big leagues. He doesn't think I can reach any of the dreams or goals I set out to do.* Instead, I chose to do what has helped me countless times in my career: I thought outside the box. *Okay, so this particular big-shot agent didn't want to work with me. That's okay. There are other ways and other people to work with in this big world.* I knew I just needed to keep plugging away—to keep doing excellent work at *Inside Edition*, keep meeting people, and keep putting myself in situations where I could learn and grow.

And almost exactly two years later, I was offered the chance to cover *Thursday Night Football* on CBS. How did that happen? Well, looking back, I see it was combination of hard work, hustling, maintaining a positive attitude, networking, God's blessing, and taking a risk.

Change, Risk, and Faith

In the television industry, most companies want you to be exclusive with them. They lock you into a very tight contract with little opportunity to work for someone else unless they approve the project. That was the case with all of my previous television jobs.

Back when I was a reporter for the local CBS station in San Antonio, I heard about a TV hosting workshop being offered by a Hollywood casting director named Marki Costello. She is the granddaughter of the legendary Lou Costello of Abbott and Costello fame. I had always wanted to learn more about hosting, so I flew to Dallas for her one-day workshop. (To this day I love taking workshops. They are never a waste of time for me. I always learn something. I have heard that even the best actors in Hollywood never stop taking acting classes.)

Marki is known for discovering and employing very effervescent and engaging on-air hosts like Jason Kennedy of *E! News*. In addition to learning her best tip on hosting and reading scripts for Marki to critique, she said something that caught my attention. She said, "When you sign those contracts, remember that exclusivity is key. That is way more important than money or perks." I did not understand what that meant at the time. In fact, I even emailed her about it afterward, trying to get more insight. In her typical Marki fashion, she emailed back and said, "Get a lawyer, sweetie." I quickly learned what she meant was *You are young, and in this dog-eat-dog world, you need to understand what all this negotiating means and always seek wise legal counsel.* It would be several years before I really came to appreciate why she'd said this. I did get a hint of its value, though, after I had worked for *Inside Edition* for four years and my contract was up. At the time, the industry was experiencing some growing pains. Budgets were tight as television was competing more and more with online shows, Netflix, and hundreds of cable channels.

During my contract renegotiation, my boss asked if I would consider moving from full-time reporter to part-time. Our show had another reporter who was working part-time, and they wanted me to consider being the second. What's important to know about this time in my life was that I loved my job at *Inside Edition*, but I desperately wanted to challenge myself creatively. Whether it was acting projects, hosting other shows, or producing, I wanted the freedom to pursue these options on my days off.

But, until that moment, all my work contracts had been exclusive, which meant I could not work for anyone else without the approval of my boss. Furthermore, due to my full-time work schedule, any opportunities were difficult to pursue, let alone ask my boss for permission to accept if an opportunity arose. But a move to part-time would mean my new contract with *Inside Edition* would be nonexclusive: I would be able to work for anyone and any company at any time.

I felt overwhelmed and a little scared. I knew this is what I wanted to do, but when it was suddenly right in front of me, I was nervous. I came home and relayed the conversation to my husband. He was excited. In fact, I remember him saying, "No kidding! This is great! It's exactly what you wanted!" I got a similar response from my agent at the time. These reactions helped tremendously. Both of these people knew my dreams and goals, and they saw it fitting right into the plan. But I was still nervous. Leaving a solid, full-time contract also meant leaving financial security. Yet the move was safe in the sense that I wasn't taking any risks. I could always go back to my boss and beg him to let me return to full-time. I wanted to take risks, but maybe not quite yet!

But when we take risks, our dreams can become reality, my friends. I remembered what Marki had told me about exclusivity, so I recognized this as my golden opportunity. Looking back now, I call my contract renegotiation one of those walk-on-water moments. Remember in Matthew 14, when the disciples were on a boat and a storm rolled in, rocking the boat and terrifying them? Then Jesus appeared, walking on the water toward the boat, and told Peter to step out of the boat and walk toward Him. Jesus asked Peter to step out in faith and take a risk, to leave the safety of the boat and try to do something impossible. Taking that kind of step is scary, and it's uncomfortable. The boat is what Peter knew: it was familiar and easy to be there. But when he took that first step, he did the unthinkable: he actually walked on water!

Taking risks are those moments in life when you can remain in the boat, but you take a chance and step out on the water instead. Going part-time was scary, but I knew if I wanted to grow—and if I wanted to pursue my dreams—I needed to take that step of faith. I felt God calling me to trust Him. As I walked, I felt Him confirming that I needed to pursue this new contract situation. I felt Him telling me that new adventures and new projects would come, but I needed to trust Him along this new path.

So I finally overcame my nervousness, stepped out of the boat, and went part-time with *Inside Edition*. It was a turning point in my career.

Ordinary Encounter, Big Opportunity

There was a plus to my part-time situation that was very appealing. I had a ten-month-old baby, and going part-time gave me more time with my son. It was a wonderful thing for a few precious months. But then reality kicked in. Here we were, living in New York City, paying an obscene amount for rent, and I had just moved from full-time reporter to part-time. Eventually our finances necessitated I get that second job, that gig I had been dreaming about.

At first, I was unsure how to use my newfound freedom to my advantage. I had plenty of dreams and ideas, but few people knew I was available. Again, it's pretty common in the broadcasting world to have an exclusive contract. And most people in the industry know it, so they wouldn't assume I was available to work other gigs. So sometimes you need to just put one foot in front of the other and start telling people your status and ideas. I did that in a very literal sense.

I was walking down the street in New York City, and I literally ran into Kurt Davis, my former boss and a vice president at CBS. He had been the news director at the local CBS affiliate in San Antonio who hired me as reporter/anchor for the station where I worked for three years prior to *Inside Edition*. He is a straight shooter and a no-nonsense kind of man. Not only do I love this in a boss, but as my mentor, I always knew exactly where I stood with Kurt. I listened when he critiqued me, and I knew his compliments were not just fluff. He meant what he said, good and bad. For this very reason Kurt caught the eye of David Rhodes, president of CBS News, and was hired to move to NYC to oversee CBS Newspath, the news division of all the CBS affiliates.

So there we were, on a street corner in NYC. He asked how I was doing and how work at *Inside Edition* was going. I didn't mince words. I said, "Kurt, it's great. And now I'm actually working part-time so I can pursue some other projects. I am free to work for other companies now, too, and I'm figuring out what that means and how I can grow my brand." Kurt listened and nodded but didn't say much in response. We chatted about a few other things and said good-bye.

As I walked away, I thought, *Oh gosh, I shouldn't have just blurted out all my dreams to Kurt. I should have just said, "Work is great at* Inside Edition; *I'm happy and doing well.* For some reason, I was worried that this former boss of mine might think I was unhappy at *Inside Edition* and therefore looking for another job, that I was not committed, and that I was flaky. Even though I had been very positive in our conversation, I was just not used to my situation yet. It felt weird to be so available.

That night I told my husband about the conversation and reiterated how I felt. He listened and said, "Well, Meg, you've wanted to pursue other projects now for a while. You want to grow your brand. And now you have the contractual freedom to do so. But if you don't talk about it and share your availability, how on earth are people going to know?"

Little did I know, he was exactly right. We prayed about the situation, and I asked God to take away my anxiety and continue to guide me.

About four months later I was walking down the street and literally bumped into Kurt again. He was on the phone so we just quickly waved and both continued on. Later that day, I got an email from Kurt. He wanted to meet with me and share an idea that I might be interested in. When we met, he told me CBS television had just picked up the rights to broadcast eight *Thursday Night Football* games that fall. He was looking to hire a correspondent to cover those games and deliver reports to all the local CBS affiliates across the country. He said he was very far into the casting process and about to hire someone when he had seen me, and remembered from our earlier meeting on that street corner in NYC that I was contractually available and eager to try new things. Would I like the job?

Moving from Safety to Trust

I left his office and immediately said a prayer of thanks to God. No matter what happened, I needed to thank the Lord for this opportunity. It's a natural tendency to immediately call our friends or family in these moments, good or bad, but I always try to take a few minutes to talk to God first. I sometimes forget, but I do believe He needs to be the first to hear my news—good and bad.

Then I called my husband and told him about the opportunity. He was so excited for me! I was going to get paid to cover the NFL? He couldn't believe it. He was so proud of me and wanted me to take the job. We talked about what it would mean for our family. My son had just turned two years old, and I would be away from him during those eight games. We talked through it and decided the opportunity was too good to pass up—and it was nice it was only for eight weeks.

I shared the news with my parents, and they helped me weigh the pros and cons as well. They said they would support whatever decision I made, but they were thrilled for me when I accepted. They knew how much I loved a challenge and thought this was a perfect opportunity.

My friends, I would have never gotten the opportunity to cover the NFL if I had not stepped out of the boat.

I did approach my boss at *Inside Edition* and ask for his approval.

Even though I did not need his permission because NFL games were on Thursday nights and I worked for *Inside Edition* Monday through Wednesday, I wanted to pursue projects that didn't interfere with my current job and to make sure my boss felt appreciated and included. He gave me his blessing and said he was super excited for me. He said he would incorporate some coverage of the games on *Inside Edition*. He also saw the value in this incredible opportunity, and I made sure he knew I would be a team player—and I was. There were a few games where I did interviews and reports for all the CBS stations, and then I would record something specifically for *Inside Edition*. It made for a lot of work and long hours, but it was important to me to keep and show my commitment and passion to deliver for both jobs.

I had an amazing experience covering the NFL for CBS for two years. Professionally, it was all I'd hoped it would be, and more. But, personally, it did have some rough patches. It was hard to be away from my family those extra days. My husband and I were forced to communicate better than ever. We had our fair share of fights and disagreements. He was cleaning up spilt milk and wiping my son's nose while I was reporting from the stadiums of NFL teams all across the country. I came home tired and went back on the road tired. I remember one particular night, when I was getting ready to head to the airport and my sweet little two-year-old looked me in the eyes and said, "Mama, I don't want you to leave today. Please stay." His soft little voice broke my heart. I went over to him and hugged him close and kissed his head. I explained I needed to go, but I would be back soon. And then I said what has become our little phrase: "We can handle that!" He smiled and snuggled up close. But it wasn't easy! That was *hard*. I had to go. I had made a commitment to the job. So I left. I know all working parents feel those tug-of-war moments. The job had incredible highs, but that was a very low point.

I went back to God and prayed He would help me and sustain me for the rest of the games. God confirmed with me that He wanted me in this job and that He had called me "for such a time as this" (Esther 4:14 NIV). Whenever I prayed about it, I would say, *Lord, please either open this door wide or close it hard.* And so far He has continued to open it wide and give me opportunities. I keep praying and asking Him almost daily. Philippians 4:6–7 says, "Do not be anxious about anything, but in every situation, by prayer and petition, with thanksgiving, present your requests to God. And the peace of God, which transcends all understanding, will guard your hearts and your minds in Christ Jesus (NIV)." Listen, this is easier said than done, but I will trust. I will keep making those requests to God for confirmation. And I still love the job! I love the rush of walking out on the field during warmups and feeling the energy, excitement, and emotion of an NFL game. There is nothing like it. Still, I will always be dealing with real-life issues as well.

Taking risks and working through struggles moves us from safety to trust. And isn't that what personal growth is all about?

Your Boat

Are you sitting in your boat right now, anxious to try something new but hesitant about taking that first step? Is Jesus calling to you from the water? Friends, I know it's scary. I've been there. But as I look back on those moments in my life, I am so glad I stepped out because God has blessed me and taught me so many new things. So trust in Him if He is telling you to step.

And always keep your eyes on Him. Remember what happened to Peter when he took his eyes off Jesus? When Peter looked down at the water, he saw a huge storm with violent waves. He was scared, and he started sinking. My industry can be the same way. When I take my eyes off Jesus, I notice the high waves and hungry sharks! But when I keep my eyes on my Savior and Lord, I get the opportunity to do things I never thought possible.

Takeway

1. Listen to your heart. Is it telling you to pursue your dreams? Is it telling you to change jobs?

2. Ask God for wisdom and providence as you pursue those dreams. Share your dreams. I started talking: I told Kurt about my desire to pursue new opportunities and that I was available. Find people in your life with whom you can share your dreams and the news of your availability. And be on the lookout. Making the life-changing connection may be as simple as walking into someone on the street!

3. When you do take that leap of faith, be respectful and gracious to those you are already working with. I kept my boss at *Inside Edition* informed of the NFL gig because I wanted him to know he was important to me and I respected him. Are you including others in the unfolding of your dreams? What can you do to make others feel important and respected?

4. When you step out of the boat, keep your eyes on Jesus. And realize it will be an ongoing, every-day, every-minute process. Some days are going to be tough. There will be moments that make you wonder what you're doing and why. But when you keep focused on Jesus, He will confirm your steps and walk with you.

*A*s an NFL quarterback, I am living out my lifelong dream of playing professional sports. I have worked hard to get here, and I am grateful to be here. As a believer, I feel God has led me to this opportunity. When I play, I am using my talents to glorify Him!

The NFL is a phenomenal platform, and I am aware of the impact that we, as players, can have on young people. Sports can teach us all a great deal about discipline, teamwork, how to win with humility, and how to graciously accept defeat. In this chapter, Megan shares about the world of NFL media coverage as well as the many lessons that can be learned from working in one of the largest sports leagues in the world.

I am convinced that God is at work in the NFL. I can't wait to see what He does next!

—Kirk Cousins, QB, Washington Redskins

Eight

Covering the NFL

Playing Ball in the Big Leagues

Winning means you're willing to go longer,
work harder, and give more than anyone else.
—VINCE LOMBARDI

*W*EEK IN AND WEEK OUT, NFL games are the most watched television events in America. In 2014, thirty-four out of the thirty-five most watched fall TV shows were NFL games. Americans love their football! And a few years ago, I got a chance to start covering the most popular professional (and some would say influential) sport in America.

The first game I covered for *Thursday Night Football* on CBS was September 11, 2014. It was memorable for a variety of reasons. First, it was in Baltimore: the Baltimore Ravens vs. the Pittsburgh Steelers, a longtime divisional rivalry.

Second—as I mentioned earlier—the game was just a few days after the Ray Rice scandal had broken. Running back for the Ravens, Rice had been caught on videotape punching his then fiancée, Janay. TMZ had gotten a hold of the video and posted it online, to the horror of the world. The NFL had responded by suspending Ray for two games, but the outcry from the public was immediate and angry. As that video footage played over and over on television and computer screens, people felt that two games was not enough.

Then, fueling the fans' passion, musical guest Rihanna was slotted as the kickoff performer for this first *Thursday Night Football* game. Several years prior photos had surfaced of Rihanna with her face bruised and battered as a result of her own domestic violence incident with then boyfriend singer Chris Brown.

I was already nervous about my first game. I knew a fair amount about the NFL because I am a huge Seahawks fan, and I had covered several Super Bowls for *Inside Edition*, but this was different. I was going to be on air, live, for four hours at a time. *Inside Edition* is not a live show; it's a thirty-minute taped newsmagazine show. To prepare for this Thursday night gig, I had to really study the teams and thoroughly learn the positions, coaches, rivalries, and rules of the game. Then I needed to deliver it to the CBS audience in an authoritative way yet also have fun, interview fans, and bring viewers to the party. It was a daunting task.

And as the Ray Rice scandal grew in intensity, I never realized just how much it would affect my job.

A Rapid-Fire Three Hours

CBS initially wanted to keep the broadcast focused on football and just cover the game. The sports department felt the Rice incident should be mentioned but not dominate the game. The discussion trickled down to our department, and leading up to the game, my boss instructed me that my report should be 99 percent about the actual matchup and the players. But it became impossible to just mention the story and move on. People were desperate for a discussion about domestic violence and about how the NFL—and specifically NFL commissioner Roger Goodell—was handling it. People also wanted to talk about how the fans were reacting.

I flew to Baltimore on Wednesday night, the day before our kick-off game. When I landed, my producer called and said, "Well, we think you should be prepared to talk more about the Ray Rice story if the stations ask." That night I don't think I slept. Instead, I did my homework and read what people were saying about the scandal, how the NFL was responding, how the leadership of the Ravens was responding, and what other key figures in the sports world were saying. I was nervous, but I still had no idea what was ahead. I had only a vague idea of how big this story was and how it would play out the next day.

On Thursday, at 4:00 p.m., I went live from M&T Bank Stadium, where the Ravens play, and I did not go off air until 7:25 p.m. that night when the pregame show took over with CBS anchor James Brown. During those three hours every CBS affiliate in the country—more than one hundred local stations—took or aired my reports. Of those one hundred, sixty would take me live, which meant reserving a two- to three-minute block of their broadcast for me to report live from the stadium. So, from 4:00 until 7:25, I would be talking, every few minutes, to a different local news or sports anchor around the country. As I cycled through the stations, literally everyone asked me about Ray Rice. They asked about latest news from Baltimore: How was the team handling losing their star player because of the scandal? What were the fans saying? Were CBS and the NFL doing anything different that night in their presentation of the game because of the scandal?

A Changing Assignment

Minutes before I gave my first live report, at about 3:45 p.m., my team was alerted that CBS had changed the preshow dramatically. Musical guest Rihanna was supposed to open the game, but it had been canceled. Instead of airing a musical number, CBS was going to have sports anchor James Brown and news anchor Norah O'Donnell host the preshow. It would be serious and address the Ray Rice situation head-on. CBS would also run two prerecorded interviews with Commissioner Goodell along with a live interview of Ravens owner Steve Bisciotti. James Brown would lead the broadcast by addressing the issue of domestic violence in America. I had very little time to digest all this, research as much as I could, and prepare my notes before going live.

I remember starting to panic a bit. This was not how I envisioned my first day of covering live football! I also knew all the suits at CBS would be watching my reports, especially in New York, Los Angeles, Chicago—all the big markets. They would want to see how I handled the pressure of such a huge story. I closed my eyes and said a quick prayer: *Lord, please be with me today. Give me the strength to do this well. To God be the glory.*

My producer, Dave Hawthorne, my photographer, Kenny Kerbs, and director Anthony Filiaci could tell I was feeling a little apprehensive. They said, "Hey, let's just take this one city at a time." These guys are the best in the business, and that night I certainly learned why. We worked as a team. If the news changed while I was giving a report, they updated me when I had a quick break in between live shots. I could feel adrenaline kicking in, and it carried me all through those three and a half hours of live TV. When our last pregame live shot of the night was completed, I finally had a moment to catch my breath.

I was tired but energized. We had done it! I was so proud of my team. We had handled more than sixty live shots for different size markets all over the country. And we had done well, but there was little time for celebrating. My night was not over. Now I needed to head inside the stadium and watch the game from the press box. Once the game concluded, I would head outside to deliver postgame reports for all those CBS stations.

I succeeded that night because of three things. First, I called upon God for strength. Second, I was part of a great team, and we were working toward the common goal of delivering the best report possible under very stressful circumstances. Everyone was alert and communicating well. This was crucial to sustain our stamina over those long, stressful three hours of live reports. And, third, I was prepared. All those years of doing research at school, giving speeches, and performing live onstage and under pressure had paid off.

Who do you call on when you have a big day at work? Who do you look to for strength when the pressure is intense? I love asking people I admire how they face challenging circumstances. We can learn a lot from the different ways people handle those situations.

The Boys' Club

People frequently ask me how I am treated as a female covering the NFL and how I handle being in the big boys' club. I wondered the same thing myself when I first got the job. I was keenly aware that tons of male sportscasters would have killed for my position. I also knew that many people would be curious about whether I really knew my stuff. In fact, when I told one of my male friends about my new job, he said, "Oh, so you are probably just covering the halftime entertainment and fluff stuff, right?" He assumed I would not be strictly a sports reporter.

We can react in a variety of ways in situations like this. I could have snapped back at my friend and said, "Actually, yes, I am covering football, and no, not just fluff." Or I could have become intimidated and thought to myself, *He's right. Who am I kidding? I don't know football very well. Everyone will think I'm a joke.* But instead, in those moments, we need to remember why God placed us on this planet: to do good work to the best of our ability and in order to glorify Him. I smiled and said, "Actually, I am doing more sports reporting, so I am really studying up!" And then I just changed the subject. I wanted my work to speak for itself—and I became even more fired up to do better than ever. So I got to work.

No Time Wasted

In my world, time is precious, and you want to have your stuff together and organized, so you don't waste anyone's time. It's respectful and professional. I have found that people in positions of power and prestige are very sensitive about the value of time and appreciate it when others respect theirs.

During my second year of covering the NFL, we had a game in Boston: the New England Patriots vs. the Tampa Bay Buccaneers. At the time the Patriots were the defending Super Bowl champions, and we really wanted an interview with their top brass. My quick-thinking producer, Anthony, and I spotted Robert Kraft, the owner of the Patriots, making his way to the stadium but stopping for an interview with the NFL network.

Mr. Kraft runs several very successful businesses and oozes self-confidence, always wearing a crisp suit and his signature tennis shoes, as he moves along with a large entourage.

Since Anthony and I were in between reports, I said to Anthony, "Why don't you go over there and ask if we can have an interview? It never hurts to ask." I adamantly believe this: No ask-y, no get-ty. I wanted to ask for the interview myself, but I had to stay in position and be camera ready for the full three hours. The longest break I got into between live shots was about ten minutes, and because I was plugged in—I was wearing an earpiece and a microphone that were both connected to my camera—I literally could not leave my spot. For three hours I could not even take a break to go to the bathroom! So Anthony, who is always up for a challenge, walked over to Mr. Kraft's entourage and waited. When he saw a moment, he made the big ask. Mr. Kraft said, "Sure, I love CBS. I'll come over in a minute. But I don't have too much time."

Anthony looked back at me and gave me a thumbs-up. I returned the signal and then immediately gave my photographer and producer a pep talk. "Guys, Robert Kraft has agreed to an interview. But the minute he walks over, we need to have our stuff in order. He won't wait, and we have to be ready. This is a big get. Let's do this right."

Sure enough, when Mr. Kraft walked over, he was impatient and did not want to wait. But we had to wait a few moments for our Chicago station to take our live shot—and I had told Mr. Kraft that it would only be a few seconds. Even a few seconds was pushing it for him. I could tell this man was not used to waiting for anyone. I looked at my photographer and let him know—without saying a word because my eyes said it all—"We need to do this, now!" He nodded, totally aware of the situation.

Mr. Kraft looked at me and said quietly, "I need to do this soon. Hundreds of people are waiting on me." At that moment our Chicago station dialed in and tossed to me—they gave a brief into and then introduced me to their Chicago audience—and I immediately started my interview with Mr. Kraft. It went great as we chatted about the weather (Boston is notorious for rough fall weather, wind, rain, and cold, and the night had cleared up beautifully) and I asked him about being the defending Super Bowl champs and how they were feeling. The interview felt seamless, there were no awkward pauses, and I had a nice, easy rapport with Mr. Kraft. It felt really good. At the end of our interview, Mr. Kraft shook my hand not once, but twice (he had started to walk away but turned back for one more handshake), and I knew we had impressed him. I felt proud of my team and texted my boss at CBS in New York City. "We got Mr. Kraft! Great interview!" My boss texted back that he was very happy. He knows what a big deal Mr. Kraft is and what a big get that was. I also knew that if I had asked Mr. Kraft a silly question or appeared unprepared, it could have damaged the whole CBS brand, not just my crew and me.

In the NFL, everyone puts in the hard work. Players go to training camp and work their hearts out. They show up prepared, they know their plays, and they deliver. If they don't, they won't make it and will most certainly get cut. Coaches know that they must develop a team that will win games. Owners know that having a winning team will result in ticket sales as well as business and social opportunities. And the NFL understands it must promote the games as well as develop relationships with brands that will benefit all the investors involved with the teams. Everyone works hard, and I do, too. In fact, I believe God calls us to work hard no matter what job we are doing.

Always More to Learn

People ask me all the time, "How do you get the job you have? How do you get to the big leagues?" I asked CBS sports anchor Jim Nantz, the best in the business, the same question. He responded, "There is always more to learn. I am never completely prepared." So Jim always gets to town a few days before a game, and he reads as much as he can about each player. That way he always has something to say. If you listen to Jim and Phil Simms during a game, they rarely have any silence; they always have something to talk about, a story to share about a player, or a direct reference to the game.

Super Bowl 45 in Arlington, Texas, was my first Super Bowl. As I walked around the stadium watching Dan Marino, Deion Sanders, and Michael Strahan broadcasting, I was in awe. I remember attending my first press conference. It was about the Super Bowl halftime show, that year featuring the Black Eyed Peas. I sat near the back of the ballroom that was already filled with press, almost to capacity. I felt like an outsider, like someone who didn't really have the right to be there. I very tentatively raised my hand to ask a question and finally got noticed. I was probably the twentieth person to ask a question that day, and I spoke hesitantly and without my usual confidence. I felt in over my head.

But I took the opportunity to observe my fellow reporters. I noticed who was in the front row and who was getting called on first. After the press conference was over, I chatted up a former CNN sports reporter and asked about the pecking order. He gave me some very important advice: "It really comes down to who wants it the worst. Some of these guys show up two or three hours before the press conference starts. They have also gotten to know the NFL personnel, and that makes it easier for them to get called on." Great information, but when I left Super Bowl 45 that year, I never expected my boss would send me back the next year. Usually *Inside Edition* rotates reporters to cover the Super Bowl.

But my boss asked me to go again. And again. For six years—and counting. And every year I've gone, I've gotten a little more comfortable. I did start showing up early to all the press conferences, and I have gotten to know the NFL officials. The big moment for me came in 2015. It was Super Bowl 49, the Seahawks vs. the Patriots. By that point, I knew what was required to play with the media big boys.

What a Rush!

On the Friday before the Super Bowl, the head coaches of each team hold a press conference in the morning—and it's a big deal. The presser is live on ESPN and the NFL networks; sometimes the national networks—CBS, NBC, and ABC—take it live as well. The Super Bowl trophy sits on a table between the opposing coaches, and the NFL makes a big show of introducing them. It's the last relaxed setting before the big game. This year the press conference featured Seahawks coach Pete Carroll and Patriots coach Bill Belichick. Both teams had won the Super Bowl very recently: the Seahawks won Super Bowl 48 the year before, and the Patriots, in 47. The room was packed with press. I had shown up super early and gotten my name on the list. (A spokesperson for the NFL compiles a list of names and media outlets in attendance, and if you make it on the list, it's pretty much a guarantee you will be called on.)

I knew my name was near the top, but I wasn't sure when I would get called on. The NFL welcomed everyone, and the press conference began. The first person they called was Tony Ventrella, a popular sports anchor from Seattle. He asked a basic question about how each of the teams was feeling. Then the NFL spokesperson pointed to me, in the front row, and said, "Megan Alexander?" Someone ran a microphone over to me. I took a deep breath, smiled, and asked my question. Me! I was called on second! The reporter from the entertainment magazine *Inside Edition*! It was a rush!

I asked Pete Carroll about Richard Sherman, a key defensive player for the Seahawks. His girlfriend was nine months pregnant and due to have their baby any day. I asked what the game plan was if she went into labor. And if you think this is a silly question, keep this in mind: countless players have had kids born right around the Super Bowl. In fact, Sherice Brown, the wife of Tim Brown of the Raiders, told me she had twins the day after her husband played in the Super Bowl in 2003. So it's a legitimate question! Think about it: What would you do? Play in the Super Bowl or watch your baby's birth? It's a spot no one wants to be in! And no coach wants to lose a key player for the Super Bowl, but neither does that coach want to tell a key player he can't be present for the birth of his child. Pete gave a great answer about supporting Richard in whatever decision he made should the situation arise. And it didn't. He played and Sherman's girlfriend did not go into labor during the Super Bowl.

But there I was, second that day to ask a question in the press conference. That little girl from five years ago at Super Bowl 45 in Dallas who had felt so insecure? I had watched, observed, learned, studied, and practiced. And I realized I deserved to be there just as much as anyone else in the press.

When I was called on, I didn't stumble because I was ready, but it had taken me several years to get to that point. Don't forget that expertise isn't developed overnight. And during that long process, the world likes to tell us we aren't good enough to reach our goals. Remember the friend who joked that I surely couldn't be covering sports? His comment could have really hurt my confidence, and I wouldn't have been nearly as determined to ask questions at a press conference. I might have just sat there, thinking, *Who am I to ask a question in this room full of sports reporters?* But I didn't; I rose to the challenge, and did excellent work. I experienced what the apostle Paul wrote about: "Pay careful attention to your own work, for then you will get the satisfaction of a job well done" (Galatians 6:4 NLT).

Fumbles Will Happen

People, especially young girls, like to ask me if I ever experienced any sexism as a female sports reporter. I am proud to say, no, not really. I think a lot of that has to do with your confidence and your performance. Sure, I never played football, so I would never be able to relate to men on that level, but I've found if I know my stuff and perform well, the men I work with are fine with females working alongside them.

However, I did learn my lesson on really doing my homework. Remember that first *Thursday Night Football* game I covered, the Ravens and the Steelers? Well, I was so focused on Ray Rice that I did not study the other players as thoroughly as I should have and later did. One of the stations had their sports anchor interview me that night. He asked me what I thought of a defensive lineman on the Ravens team, C. J. Mosley, and how I thought he would match up against Washington. The only thing I knew was that C. J. had graduated from Alabama. That's it! Fumble! I quickly responded with a general answer about the Ravens and then started talking about something else.

I always felt like that sports anchor had tried to test me that night, to see if I really knew my stuff, and I had failed the test. I was mad at myself for not having more to say. And I promised myself I would be more prepared the next time. But in reality, we are human, and we will have those fumbles. It's life. We can only do our best and move on.

Whatever task is right in front of you today, do it to the best of your ability. And when people make comments or you feel insecure, don't compare yourself to them or to others. Be as prepared as you can be and do your own best work. Work hard, and know that at the end of the day, we are responsible for ourselves. Covering Thursday night games for the NFL taught me these valuable lessons, and I have the opportunity to see very talented athletes and successful businessmen in action. And competition is healthy! It can sharpen and bring out the best in us. I got the chance to observe the best NFL players, coaches, owners, and sports broadcasters in action, and I gained tremendous respect for the way they play in the "big leagues."

Takeaway

I've learned a few things playing in the big leagues that I think are invaluable in any industry:

1. Time is of the essence. Respect other people's time, and they will respect yours.

2. Have your stuff organized. Be prepared. Put in the necessary hard work beforehand. Know what you are doing and do it.

3. Be professional. No complaining and no excuses.

4. Work as a team. My producer, photographer, and I needed to work as a tight unit to pull off our football assignments.

*A*s a cold-case detective, I've often struggled to understand God's plan in the midst of the terrible crimes I've investigated. Many of these cases ended up on *Dateline,* where believers and unbelievers alike were exposed to the darkest recesses of human behavior. My Christian worldview helped me survive some of these difficult investigations and understand the nature of humans, especially the suspects I investigated. In the end, I realized these men and women were really no different from any of us, myself included.

We are all fallen, imperfect creatures in need of a Savior. But for the grace of God, any of us might find ourselves tempted to act according to our fallen nature. As I remembered the grace God extended to me, it was much easier to extend grace to others, including the people I had to take to jail.

In this chapter, Megan explores the honest feelings and struggles she encountered when she had to report on some unsavory crimes and sensational stories. Learning the specific details at each crime scene or event is no fun and certainly not glamorous. Like me, she found that her Christian worldview helped her navigate each difficult situation. She remembered the entourage of Jesus, filled with prostitutes, tax collectors, and other immoral criminals. This chapter is an honest and authentic discussion about glorifying God in *all* we do.

—J. Warner Wallace, author of *Cold Case Christianity* and *God's Crime Scene*

Nine

Tiger Woods

The Dark Corners of the Spotlight

*So let's not get tired of doing good. At just the right time
we will reap a harvest of blessing as long as we don't give up.*

—GALATIANS 6:9

THE HEADLINES ARE OFTEN DOMINATED with sensational and often vulgar stories. Why? Because of human nature. Sadly, the media knows and caters to the voyeuristic nature of the general public, who want the sordid details of the private lives and failings of celebrities.

I've covered my share of the salacious more times than I care to count. One of the more memorable moments was when the best-known golfer in the world was caught cheating on his wife. Yup. Tiger Woods. And he didn't cheat with just one woman. As the story unfolded, the media reported twenty-seven mistresses and counting.

Here I was, a churchgoing, TobyMac-listening, Beth Moore–reading newlywed who had just moved to NYC for her big national media job. I was excited to prove to my boss—and the world—that I was a great reporter.

When the Tiger Woods scandal broke, my spirit was tested. And I thought I wanted to quit.

Scandals and Affairs

First, I had known I would encounter these types of stories. I watched TV. I'd seen the covers of the grocery store magazines. I knew this was part of my professional world. But I had not yet been assigned to the big scandal when it broke; I had not yet had to cover a scandal in great detail for weeks at a time.

I almost equate this kind of journalistic work to that of a homicide detective. We all know bad things happen, but most people usually just read the headline—So-and-so was arrested today for XYZ—and then they move on, never giving it another thought. The detective, however, has to spend weeks learning every detail, seeing every picture, and reliving every aspect of the crime.

Similarly, my job was to investigate. And as the mistresses started coming forward and sharing personal details of their encounters with Tiger Woods, I wanted to cover my eyes and my ears and run away. I didn't want to know if Tiger Woods was good in bed! And yet everyone from TMZ, *Today*, CNN and yes, *Inside Edition* was asking intimate questions and reporting all the lurid details of his affairs.

So what do you do when your boss sends you to interview the mistresses? I mean, what journalism class prepares you for that interview? There I was, a young reporter, eager to prove myself, interviewing call girls and pimps.

Don't worry. I won't rehash the details here. Frankly, I'd rather never think about some of these interviews again. But I do want to mention that I could have avoided sharing this experience in this book. It would've been easier to leave it out. I could have just described the inspiring and exciting moments of my career: covering the Super Bowl, interviewing Oprah, or working out with "Stone Cold" Steve Austin. But that's not the whole picture of what I do.

Those are only *some* of the assignments I get, and I want to be truthful about the realities of being a believer in my industry and how my faith has been challenged. And the Tiger Woods scandal was a trying time.

God's Light and the World's Darkness

Perhaps you have been in a similar situation. . . .

Maybe you are a lawyer and had to represent a client you felt was guilty of a crime that was terribly unpleasant. Or you are the human relations director who has to deal with complaints every day. So how do we get through these unpleasant and trying times? I've learned a lot has to do with my approach and my attitude. And I remember the verse "Call upon Me in the day of trouble" (Psalm 50:15).

Regarding Mr. Woods, it was not my job to judge. Sure, I felt uncomfortable. Sure, I wanted to tell the world what a scumbag Tiger was and how horrific he was to treat women this way. Even more, I wanted to have nothing to do with this story! In fact, I could have said no to my boss and not covered the story. But it was already day 20 of the scandal, and it was not going away. If I said no to this assignment, another difficult one would come. I realized I needed to develop a strategy for handling these types of stories. The Tiger Woods story wouldn't be the last of its kind that I would be assigned.

I've always prayed that God will guide me and that I will hear His voice. I did not sense God telling me to turn down the assignment that day. I didn't sense any restrictions at all. So I took it on. I've come to realize that living out my faith at work doesn't always mean rejecting every job I will struggle with as a follower of Christ. I do good work, and I don't compromise my values, but I pick and choose my battles. Sometimes I just need to do my job.

So I got to work covering the Tiger Woods scandal. At one point,

I was sent to Howard Stern's studio in Manhattan. Howard Stern is known as the shock jock of radio. He says pretty much whatever he wants on air, and that means cursing, lewd stories, and more. He was interviewing three of Tiger Woods's mistresses, holding a "Tiger Woods Mistresses Beauty Pageant," and asking about every intimate and salacious detail imaginable. He had invited members of the media to his very spacious studio in midtown Manhattan to be his audience for the show. That day, as I watched these three women—wearing bikinis—report on every intimate detail about their time with Tiger, a song kept running through my head. It was one I had learned in Sunday school as a child: "Oh, be careful, little ears, what you hear. Oh, be careful, little eyes, what you see." Oh, how I did not want to be in that studio.

Now, let me be clear: I am not bashing Howard Stern. He is entitled to free speech, and he has a talent for what he does. He has a huge audience, and some people love his style. But God gives us free will to choose what we say, do, watch, read, and listen to. It's my personal conviction that some of the topics discussed on his radio show are not beneficial to my spirit. I just don't find Howard Stern's radio show appealing, and that is my personal opinion. I have good friends who love him, and that is their choice. But I want to be the best person I can be, and for me that means I will listen to people other than Howard Stern. My choice.

But there I was, sitting in Howard Stern's audience, listening to his show as a Sunday school song ran through my head. I prayed I would be salt and light in the situation, and I found a brief opportunity before Stern went on the air. One of the producers came around with a microphone, interviewing the press in the audience. She held the microphone up to me and asked something to the effect of "Will your publication be leading with this story? How big of a deal is Howard's interview with these mistresses?" Other reporters had responded with comments like "This is a big story! Everyone wants to know all the details about Tiger Woods and all his mistresses," or "Only Howard can ask anything and everything." When the producer came to me, I took a deep breath and said something to the effect of "This is a big story because the public sees a superstar whose marriage has crumbled, and people are wondering why. They look at his beautiful wife and children and life and wonder why he risked the heartache and pain. What made him and these women decide to engage?" The producer nodded and moved on.

I realize I'd said nothing profound. But I was desperately trying to steer the conversation away from the sensational and toward a more significant discussion of human nature, sin, and the public's fascination with scandal. I did nothing earth-shattering. I was trying to follow my convictions and make this story more about human nature and less about vapid details. At the end of the day, the vapid details dominated the story. But I did try to ask questions that went a little deeper.

Sex and Politics

Guess what? Another story came along that also tested my spirit greatly: the Eliot Spitzer scandal. Breaking news revealed that the then governor of New York had hired numerous prostitutes from an elite escort service, all while he was married. The FBI caught him when they investigated suspicious monetary transactions. These eventually led them to the escort service. As a result of the investigation and media firestorm, Spitzer stepped down as governor.

The entire media world covered the story extensively, and once again I was asked to take the story and report on all the salacious details. The media was obsessed with finding a particular call girl who had taken down the governor. This quest led me to a loft apartment in New York City, where the city's so-called but former King of Pimps lived. The nickname stuck even though he was technically no longer a pimp after being busted some years prior. Because the call girl had previously worked for him, my show wanted to interview him. They wanted to know about the call girl, how the business worked, and anything the public would be shocked to learn.

As with the Tiger Woods story, I could have said no to the assignment. But the Spitzer story unfolded for several weeks, and it required many other interviews. If I had said no to the King of Pimps, I would likely have been asked to cover a different aspect of the story. And if I said no over and over again, I would likely have been fired. My job was to cover the news, and this was the news. I knew going into the job that I would encounter assignments like this, and if I didn't like it, I would probably do well to find another profession.

So my crew and I walked into his penthouse apartment that day, and we all shook his hand, just as we would any other interview subject. His apartment was very modern and professional looking. (I guess I expected it to look more like a nightclub!) He gave me an evil smile, and my stomach turned. (I didn't even want to be talking to this man!) He offered me a glass of water, and I politely declined. I just wanted to get this over with. But I kept it professional and tried very hard to treat him as I would anyone else, even though my skin was crawling as I sat a few feet away from this sleazeball. I really wanted to yell at him for taking advantage of young women and treating sex—something I believe to be a gift from God—so lightly, so disrespectfully, so wrongly.

Oh, I was definitely uncomfortable, but I did my job and asked the questions my boss wanted me to ask. And the King of Pimps gave me his programmed answers about how women do this of their own free will and can actually make very good money. He even tried to glamorize the lifestyle. (I wanted to debate him on that!) The only time I made a comment in response to his was when he said all the girls put their health first by carrying condoms and insisting the men use them at all times. I stated that abstinence is a better choice if you really want to put your health first and if you truly value your body. Aside from that remark, I did my job and left.

I will say, I went home that night feeling defeated. This was the story I was putting my journalistic talents to use for? It was hard! I prayed that the media would lose interest in this story and we would all move on. But the public kept clicking on the Eliot Spitzer saga. In turn, the media kept giving the public more of what it wanted. That's where you, dear reader, come in. People often ask me why the media covers the Kardashians so much. I usually respond by asking, "Do you ever buy a magazine with their faces on the cover? Or ever watch their show? If so, then you are telling the media you want more."

You, readers, hold more power than you realize. If you don't like something, don't click on it—change the channel instead! Disinterest sends a clear signal to the media because ratings rule the game. If no one pays attention to a story or program, it doesn't get high ratings, so the media moves on.

Small Conversations, Big Impact

Maybe I didn't feel at the time like I was doing anything profound. I was covering a story and doing exactly what my boss had asked me to do. But I was looking for ways to make an impact, to be salt and light in a dark and ugly situation. But that kind of situation is where God can really move, and the hope that He will do so makes those rough days and sordid stories a little bit more bearable for me. I did see God work as the Eliot Spitzer story developed because it shed light on the dark industry of prostitution.

My boss sent me to interview a young girl who had left college to become a full-time call girl. As she sat across from me and praised her industry and her occupation, I could sense she still was uncertain about the lifestyle she had chosen. I felt God telling me to do something, to say something. My heart started beating very fast in my chest. When the interview was over, as she was putting on her coat and everyone was leaving the room, I quietly walked back over to her, looked her in the eyes, and said softly, "Hey, you are a beautiful, talented girl. And there are other options in life for you." I pressed a small piece of paper into her hand.

The paper gave the website of a wonderful organization called Authentic Relationships International (ARI). This nonprofit organization provides support to people who have worked in or been hurt by the sex industry. Many years ago, when I was in San Antonio, I had interviewed Gene McConnell, the man who founded ARI.

The young woman thanked me, took the paper, and walked out of the room. I never heard from her again, but maybe God used me to plant a seed that day. Maybe she contacted the organization. Maybe she is no longer a call girl. That is my prayer.

Choose Your Battles

Whatever your line of work, you may find yourself bothered by an assignment you are given. First, remember you are in that situation for a reason. The reason may be just to offer a different perspective by voicing your opinion.

Still, when you are bothered by an assignment, I believe you need to make the best decision you know how. It helps me to run through this mental checklist:

1. Seek God's direction—pray and ask Him to guide you.

2. Talk to a wise friend whose advice you can trust.

3. Weigh the pros and cons of doing/saying something. Is this the right battle to fight? What could the outcome be, both good and bad?

4. Make a decision and move on. Don't second-guess yourself.

Sometimes you will feel the urge to do something, like I did after I interviewed the call girl. Sometimes you will not feel called to do anything except your job. And still at other times—in the words of Nancy Reagan—you will need to "just say no." And I have done that. . . .

God will guide you. Remember Moses feeling completely unprepared to lead his people through the desert? He had a speech impediment and very low confidence. Moses had the same doubts I had. In the Old Testament Exodus 4:1 he cried out to the Lord about his fear: "What if they do not believe me or listen to me . . ." (NIV). Sound familiar? He had the same fears and doubts you and I face every day. And guess what? God gave Moses a profound promise. In Exodus 4:12 God answered, "Now go; I will help you speak and teach you what to say" (NIV).

Even if you don't know exactly how you will handle certain situations and are scared, keep taking steps forward. I believe God wants us not only to work hard but also to be His light in the areas of influence He has given us.

✦   ✦   ✦

Before I wrap this up, I need to share about a time when covering a not-so-desirable story really did work in my favor. When famous pro wrestler Hulk Hogan and his wife got a divorce, there was a race among the entertainment newsmagazines to land that first interview with his ex-wife. *Inside Edition* ended up securing the interview first and my boss asked me to do it. I admit, asking someone about something so intimate and painful as their divorce made me more than uncomfortable, but I flew to LA and did the interview to the best of my ability.

When *Inside Edition* aired the story, the sister network of CNN, called HLN, called *Inside Edition* and asked if I would be a guest on their nightly entertainment program called *Showbiz Tonight* and discuss my conversation with the ex–Mrs. Hogan. I was so excited. CNN? HLN? I have admired and watched their programs for years. After *Inside Edition*, I headed to the CNN headquarters, which is near my office in midtown Manhattan. I still remember walking in the building and being escorted to the *Showbiz Tonight* set. I gave an interview that night and had great chemistry with the anchor of the show, A. J. Hammer. When I left, the production team asked if would be available to come on the show as a guest commentator again. I said "Of course!" This was the beginning of a three-year relationship with that network.

For almost every week for three years I was a familiar face on that program. I got the chance to give my opinion on every major entertainment headline and attempt to shine my light for Christ in how I conducted myself and what my views on stories were. *And* it was a blast. The program was canceled in 2014 after a great nine-year run. I got the chance to work with CNN and HLN because of my interview with Hulk Hogan's ex! What we think is pointless, God can use as a stepping-stone to something bigger.

Takeaway

Based on your career, your circumstances, and your sense of God's desire for you, you will need to decide for yourself what you are willing to do. It's important to think about your possible response and the consequences before the situation arises. Then, when you face a difficult decision, you have some good guidelines already in place.

1. Hard times *will* come.

2. Pray that God will clearly reveal to you what He wants you to do in a given situation.

3. Don't judge others, for we all are sinful and fall short of the glory of God (Romans 3:23).

4. Make the most of the situation you are in. Look for small opportunities to shine your light and be true to yourself. Trust that God has you there for a reason and that He will use you.

5. If you really disagree with the situation and sense God telling you not to participate, get out. But realize that your next assignment may involve the same challenging issues.

*W*hile growing up on a Mennonite farm in Dodge City, Kansas, I vividly remember a moment right before I graduated from high school. From where I was standing, I looked to my left—wheat field! I looked to my right—wheat field! I knew God had put a big dream in my heart, and even though I had little experience, I felt God calling me to Hollywood. So after I graduated, I moved there with few contacts, little direction, and big dreams. Six months after arriving, I landed a part on the CBS sitcom *Evening Shade.*

Today I'm the cofounder of Pure Flix, the largest independent faith and family studio in the world. But the road wasn't easy. There were days I found myself dressed in a purple dinosaur outfit entertaining children at birthday parties in order to pay my rent. Life isn't like a script. Things don't always work out in two hours—or even two years. But I always knew that God had a purpose for me and He was in control.

If God can lead a young man from the wheat fields of Kansas to a producer seat in Hollywood, he can help you see your dreams become a reality. Embrace the truth that your dreams aren't frivolous; in fact, your God-given dreams might just be the most important part of your life.

—David A. R. White, cofounder of Pure Flix, actor,
and author of *Between Heaven and Hollywood*

Ten

Life Does Not Always Follow a Script

Dealing with Drama

There is only one way to avoid criticism.
Do nothing. Say nothing. Be Nothing.

—ARISTOTLE

MAYBE YOU'VE HEARD THE SAYING "If people aren't being so nice to you, then you are probably doing something right." A good friend of mine who is the morning anchor on a major news channel told me this when she was dealing with some workplace drama. But, as Christians, we also discussed how, at first glance, this concept can seem foreign and very confusing. I had been taught the value of the fruit of the Spirit—love, joy, peace, patience, kindness . . . etc., and to love our neighbor as ourselves and do good to others, treating them the way we want to be treated. But when you get to the rat race of New York City, things become . . . different.

I'm not saying you need to abandon your values. No, ma'am! I fiercely believe Christian girls can succeed in the business world even if they're seen as nice girls or goody-two-shoes. I will share several examples in a moment, but first let me reassure you that, even in a rat race, you can still maintain your faith and core values. The key to that will be aligning your thoughts, words, and actions with what Jesus teaches: "Be as shrewd as snakes and as innocent as doves" (Matthew 10:16 NIV). Let me share what I have learned about being wise, how people around you will behave, and how you might choose to respond.

Jealousy on the Set

I have a good friend who is the morning traffic anchor in a major market. Let's call her Tina. She is super talented, beautiful, and in her late twenties. She moved up quickly, jumping to a large market in just a few years. She is a Christian and also prides herself on being a nice person and making friends wherever she goes. She got along easily with everyone at her news station the first year she was there.

Tina did her job well, and viewers responded. She quickly became one of the most popular morning personalities. Her news director responded by promoting her: in addition to doing traffic, he began letting her anchor the news. She started with the weekend evening slots, but eventually moved to the most coveted slot, anchoring the morning show. Tina was no longer just the traffic reporter, but a cohost on the morning telecast. She told me that suddenly her fellow cohosts, who had once been friendly and pleasant, stopped talking to her and, during commercial breaks, ignored her on the set. She also found out they went to her boss, behind her back, and complained that she was getting too much airtime.

Tina and I went to lunch, and as she shared this scenario with me, a couple of thoughts came to mind.

Turn the Other Cheek

First, you need to have thick skin to be in this business. Period. It's not for the faint of heart. This doesn't mean you need to be bulletproof or be so ice cold that you don't feel anymore, but you need to learn to let things roll off your back. Why? Keep reading.

People who work in media understand that they are there to entertain and inform, not necessarily to make friends. This principle is true in most industries. Employees are paid to get their work done, not to make friends. Sure, work friendships can be a nice benefit to any job, but it's not what earns a profit for a company. The number one reason I work at *Inside Edition* is because I am a good reporter and I deliver for my boss. Period. It's not because I'm a nice person or because I've made tons of friends here. I can and do maintain my personal morals and values at work. I also engage people and am friendly (that's part of being a good reporter), and sometimes I do forge new friendships. But I cannot forget I am there to do a job and make my company more successful, whether that is measured by viewership or ad sales.

It was with that mind-set that I listened to and tried to assess Tina's situation. Once I heard what was going on, and because I had watched Tina on the newscast, I knew her cohosts' behavior was because they felt threatened. It seemed they were insecure about their skills and jealous of her talent, her larger role in the newscast, and her new responsibilities. So these coworkers responded immaturely when they stopped talking to Tina. They knew full well that Tina, who liked people and enjoyed her cohosts, would be bothered by their icy silence. I explained to Tina what a good friend of mine, a national news anchor, had recently shared with me: "If people aren't being so nice to you at work, then you are probably doing something right." Unfortunately, in our business, that is true.

Okay, you ask, *what did I advise Tina?* I told her, "Stay true to yourself and don't let the situation change you." For Tina, that meant she would keep being her bubbly self and try to act like she didn't notice anything different about her cohosts' behavior.

I also advised her to do what an earlier boss of mine told me when

I went through a similar situation. He said, "Stay above the fray—and let this be the year of Megan." So I told Tina, "Let this be the year of Tina! Be proud of all you're doing. Sit up straight, look your best, and anchor those newscasts with confidence. Tune out those coworkers, avoid gossip, and focus on doing the best job you can. And don't stop being *you*. Keep saying hi to your coworkers even if they don't respond. And grow a thicker skin."

Thick Skin

Senator Shelley Moore Capito put it: "Having a thick skin doesn't mean that you're hard or harsh. I was lucky because I was born with a thick skin. That doesn't mean that things don't bother me, but you have to keep it in perspective."

I'm grateful for perspective, because at some point we come to realize or we decide that some of these workplace dynamics are just not worth worrying too much about. Some of these situations naturally fade. In fact, most of the time if you stop giving the problem attention—if you stop showing people that their treatment of you is getting under your skin—those people lose interest and move on. Here's some solid wisdom for anything you'll face at the office: "Be . . . slow to speak and slow to anger" (James 1:19).

My father has also managed to stay out of office politics and away from water-cooler gossip. When someone starts gossiping or acting silly, he steps into his polite but busy mode: he moves on, walks away, and focuses on something positive. I have followed my dad's example countless times in the workplace. It's amazing how quickly someone can derail your ambition with petty comments or actions. Don't let this happen. Stay focused on your goal and keep moving forward. I have found that the longer you practice this polite-but-busy approach, the easier it becomes.

My photographers, whom I work closely with, often ask me, "Hey, are you going to the farewell dinner for so and so?" I almost always respond with "That person is leaving? When was that announced?" My photographers will laugh and ask, "Oh, you didn't hear about all the drama?" And I say, "Nope! You know me, guys. I'm the last to know!" I make a joke out of it. It's my choice to stay out of the office gossip. But I don't need to make anyone else feel bad if they are participating, and I hope I never act as if I'm better than those who choose to connect over coffee and gossip. I can only do my part: I can only control myself.

A Tense Situation

I will share another story of how silly and competitive TV can be. A few years ago, in New York City, I was asked to fill in for a day on a very popular syndicated morning show. I had hosted a morning show and anchored the morning news in San Antonio for several years, so I was pretty confident I knew what I was stepping into. But you never know what personalities you might be working with.

As I was getting my hair and makeup done in the dressing room, the regular male cohost came in to say hello and introduce himself. He appeared very friendly as he told me, "We are here to make you look good and make sure you have a great time!" *How nice*, I thought. *But wait a second: this is TV, where people are not always the same on the air and off.* . . . I became unsure if he was really being truthful. I quickly realized his words were just that . . . words.

When I headed out to the set with my script, we had about fifteen minutes before we went live, so I asked him about some segments in order to gauge my chemistry with him. He was suddenly not quite so friendly. He started giving me one-word answers and was not interested in chatting. I made some notes and got prepared the best I could.

I realized I would need to just do my best and stay true to myself, to be friendly and not let his behavior affect me. Pretty soon we heard a countdown of "five . . . four . . . three . . . two . . . one!" and we were on the air. I smiled brightly, took a deep breath, prayed the Lord would ease my fears and give us a good show, and started reading the greetings from the teleprompter. Once we started the show, everything went relatively smoothly, but a couple times during one segment the male host read my lines! I saw that the teleprompter clearly said "MEGAN:" right before lines from my script and then "HIS NAME:" with lines from his script." It was as clear as day.

Now, I am a friendly and kind person, so why would he take my lines? I decided there were only two reasons this was happening: he was acting that way toward me because he felt insecure and threatened, or because this is what he always did. Since I was the fill-in host, I didn't know if the latter was true, but again, I had only one chance to figure out this on-air dance, or I might not get asked back!

"Do I Have the Right Intro?"

Then I remembered one of my good friends mentioning this had happened to her: her cohost started reading all her lines. The problem with being on a live show is you can't say anything about what is happening; you just need to roll with it. Most of us want to be professional and not act like divas by saying something like "Hey! He stole my lines!" My friend quietly approached the show's writer and mentioned the problem. The writer said he had noticed it and encouraged her to gently say something to her coworker. She did, and the situation got better.

I had ignored my cohost the first time he read my lines, but during a commercial break after he did it a second time, I loudly said, "So, I have the next intro, right? Okay, I'm all set." I wanted to let him know

I was aware of what he was doing; I wanted to assert myself. It's dumb little things like this you sometimes have to just deal with. I try to take a deep breath, assess the situation, and then move forward as confidently as possible.

When I watched the show later, I couldn't even tell there was some tension between the cohost and me—and that is something I am proud of. I don't want the audience to see that my feathers have been ruffled. I was hired to be pleasant and friendly and to banter back and forth with my cohost. This was an upbeat, lighthearted morning show. The tension may be funny in the *Anchorman* movies, but I did not want to be known for that.

You will need to choose how you will handle this kind of situation when it comes along for you.

I spoke up, and the problem was solved for the remainder of the morning. There will be times, however, when speaking up doesn't solve the problem.

To Speak or Not to Speak?

A dear friend of mine is an actor in New York City. Clayton loves to act and feels God created him for this purpose. He recently auditioned for a play and got the part. Then the writer of the play googled him—as he did all the cast members—and learned that my friend is a Christian. The writer actually asked my friend to quit his role, saying he didn't feel it was a good fit. My friend argued that his religion should not be a factor in the casting process and that he wanted his work to speak for itself. After a lot of back and forth with the director via email, however, my friend eventually walked away from the project. He began to feel it would be too hostile an environment. He would no longer be able to just put his head down and do good work. So my friend moved on.

At first, his agent gave my friend a hard time because he disagreed with his decision. His agent thought this was a good part and he should stick it out. That was hard on my friend because he didn't want to disappoint his agent or burn any business bridges. My friend had sought the advice of friends and then been careful about how he declined. He was gracious and thoughtful with his words, and stated that he simply needed to pass on this opportunity. He also had to communicate this to his agent. Even though he knew his agent initially wanted him to take the role, he had to hold true to his convictions. My friend declined the role and wished the cast and crew the best.

Well, you may have heard the expression "When God closes a door, somewhere He opens a window." When my friend walked away from that play, he was available for another project that came along almost immediately. Still, he was proud of himself for attempting to keep the role he had won. He tried, but he reached the point where it did not feel like a good fit.

To speak or not to speak? To walk or not to walk? Every situation is different. There is no one-size-fits-all approach that works for every individual. We need to pray for discernment in whatever situation we find ourselves. Sometimes we will need to walk away from a particular situation, move on, and wait for the next opportunity. There is no shame at all in that course of action.

I believe the Bible gives us some great guidance as well as encouragement about being vigilant and smart in these situations. Jesus Himself warned His followers then and us today: "I am sending you out like sheep among wolves. Therefore be as shrewd as snakes and as innocent as doves" (Matthew 10:16 NIV). In other words, be aware of the world around you. Business is tough. It is competitive. It is sometimes ruthless. But I believe you can survive and thrive if you put the above into practice.

LEFT: Third grade soccer team photo.

RIGHT AND BELOW: Winning Miss Washington Pre-teen in 1993. Then, getting to sit at the anchor desk at Channel 5 in Seattle (KING 5). My first taste of the biz—I was hooked!

ABOVE: My first billboard, the morning news team for KENS 5 in San Antonio, Texas.

ABOVE: A promotional picture as a reporter for CBS's *Thursday Night Football. Photo taken by Kristy Belcher.*

ABOVE: The *Inside Edition* team celebrating IE's 25th anniversary. To my left is the anchor, Deborah Norville, and to Deborah's left our executive producer, Charles Lachman. I work with a great team.

LEFT: On the set at *Inside Edition* in New York.

RIGHT: Interview with Deborah Norville about our choice of abstinence until our marriage. Thanks to *Inside Edition* for covering the story!

LEFT: Interviewing Jason Aldean backstage at the ACM Awards in Las Vegas.

RIGHT: Welcoming a contestant to the National American Miss pageant in Palm Springs, California. I love encouraging the next generation.

LEFT: With the incredible J. J. Watt at the CMT awards!

ABOVE: Paying it forward. A student from my high school joins me at work for a day.

ABOVE: The CBS *Thursday Night Football* team: Anthony Filiaci, Dave Hawthorne, Kenny Kerbs, me, and Kurt Davis.

LEFT: At Super Bowl 48 in New Jersey with my friend Gabby Douglas.

RIGHT: New Orleans quarterback Drew Brees dunks me with Gatorade to test out the Microsoft surface. This was a one-take wonder!

ABOVE: Filming *Heartbeats* in Mumbai, India. Incredible experience to be in a movie directed by Duane Adler.

ABOVE: Covering the Seahawks vs. 49ers game in Santa Clara, California, fall 2015.

LEFT: One of those interviews where faith and career intersect: I'm chatting with Roma Downey and Mark Burnett about *Son of God*. They would become good friends and role models.

LEFT: Just a few weeks into my job at *Inside Edition*, I'm interviewing Miss America 2008, Kirsten Haglund, just days after she won. She has become a good friend and soul sister.

RIGHT: Hosting the Inspirational Country Music Awards with my friend Storme Warren in Nashville, Tennessee. We hosted the show for five years!

RIGHT: You never know what my job will entail. This story was about getting a "Snooki makeover" with Nicole Polizzi from the show *Jersey Shore* on MTV.

LEFT: Posing with ReeShee the orangutan. I love the animal stories I cover! I'm the only reporter who has swum underwater with orangutans.

ABOVE: Taking a ride on Bubbles the elephant at the T.I.G.E.R.S. reserve in Myrtle Beach, South Carolina.

RIGHT: Taking a ride in a Black Hawk helicopter with the U.S. Army for a story on Super Bowl security in Phoenix, Arizona, for Super Bowl 49.

LEFT: My photographer Bill Viskup and I take a ride with the U.S. Coast Guard, San Jose, California.

LEFT: Announcing at the spring 2016 U.S. Women's Soccer Team SheBelieves Cup, U.S. vs. Germany, at Nissan Stadium in Nashville, Tennessee, a real girl-power moment.

LEFT: Covering Super Bowl 50 with Miss Universe, Pia Wurtzbach.

ABOVE: Dad, Mom, me, Brian, and my sister, Becky, on my wedding day, 2008.

RIGHT: My kids keep me grounded.

ABOVE: Family photo taken in Nashville, 2015. Chace (four years old), Catcher (five months old), Brian, and me.

ABOVE: Our family is not perfect, but we keep laughing! *Photo courtesy of Sarah Jones Photography.*

Getting Unstuck

So what about those times when nothing seems to be working, when no job can be had, when discouragement weighs heavily on your heart? Nothing has clicked, you are out of ideas about which doors to knock on, and you are frustrated that you just can't seem to get the job you dream of. You may be reading this and thinking, *Well, good for Megan, but I don't know where to start. I can't even start the process!* You may feel that you are stuck in your current job and can't move to the next level.

This is an important conversation. In fact, I *love* this type of conversation. First, we can remind ourselves that, more than we may realize, people in positions of power have been stuck at one point or another. Second, I think the answer to getting unstuck is less complicated than we realize. Let me illustrate this with a story.

My good friend Kirsten Haglund won Miss America in 2008. But once that year was over, she was back to square one. Are you surprised to hear this? I was, too. We assume that once someone has a great job or an incredible opportunity like being Miss America, which offers lots of travel and networking, the person will never struggle to look for another job, that he or she will be set for life. As Miss America, Kirsten made countless speaking appearances and interacted with all kinds of people from different companies and non-profits. But once her year was over, she had no full-time job offer in her preferred field.

Calvin Coolidge offers this perspective:

Nothing in the world can take the place of persistence. Talent will not; nothing is more common than unsuccessful men with talent. Genius will not; unrewarded genius is almost a proverb.

Education will not; the world is full of educated derelicts. Persistence and determination alone are omnipotent.[*]

My dad likes to summarize this as the well-known idiom "The early bird gets the worm." When he was a young broker, he would frequently be the first person to work—at 5:00 a.m.—so he was the one who turned on the lights. This early arrival showed my dad's persistence. He was determined to get in early, stay late, and work hard until he had built his business. And forty years later, now a vice president, he still occasionally turns on the lights.

Such persistence teaches that the difference between success and failure is . . . stopping. People who fail come to an obstacle in their path and simply stop. Successful people look at an obstacle and find a path around it.

I became friends with Kirsten while she was still Miss America when I interviewed her for *Inside Edition*. After we ran into each other years later at a Super Bowl party, our husbands became good friends. In fact we often spend time with Kirsten and Ryan. They are one of those couples who radiate goodness and kindness. Over dinner one night, Kirsten and I were talking about how to make it in New York City, and she shared the story of how she became the news anchor of the startup web network Styrk.com.

Showing Up

Kirsten had been feeling a bit discouraged. She had ended her year as Miss America several years earlier and could not find a full-time job. After so many months of searching, a lot of people would pack their bags and call it quits or switch careers and find another job in the city.

---

[*] www.brainyquote.com/quotes/authors/c/calvin_coolidge.html.

But Kirsten was determined to figure out how to enter the broadcasting world.

One night she was invited to a cocktail party hosted by a political speaker. When the night of the event rolled around, she was tired and not sure if she would attend. She had even already put on her pajamas! But at the last minute her husband encouraged her to go. "Maybe you will meet someone," he said. She reluctantly agreed, got dressed, and dragged herself out the door.

That night at the mixer, the speaker talked about his plans to launch a political news show for the web. When he opened it up for questions, Kirsten raised her hand and asked how he planned to include millennials. He answered that he was not yet sure. He found Kirsten at the end of the night and asked what she was doing for work. The two talked for a good while and exchanged contact info. To make a long story short, Kirsten was offered the job as the first news anchor of the web show on Styrk.com.

How did she get this job? By showing up. It's true that—as Woody Allen put it—"eighty percent of success is showing up." So go to class. Meet someone for coffee. Volunteer for a project that's connected to a business you are interested in.

My friend Anastasia Brown, author of *Be a Girl Principles* and a well-known music supervisor for major films and television shows, shared her show-up story with me. She had ended a job with a record label and was unsure about her next move. With no paying jobs available, she did something brilliant. She volunteered to direct the Nashville Film Festival for a full year. It was a strictly volunteer position, but she treated it like a full-time job. She worked on this project nine to five, sometimes more hours, every weekday. She made business cards and set up meetings. She made contacts and connections that eventually led her to a job when the year was over. This was very resourceful and creative. Plus, she had honored God with *all* of her jobs—whether paying or volunteer, because she was always working for the same Boss: "Whatever you do, work at it with all your heart, as working for the Lord" (Colossians 3:23 NIV).

After I graduated from college, my first paying job in the radio and television industry was nine dollars an hour. My next job was ten dollars an hour. This was occasionally discouraging because I could barely pay the bills. But I tell you what, those jobs built character. If I had gone straight to a well-paying job in the industry, I would not have appreciated the hard work, persistence, and dedication that it takes to get there. My first job—as a DJ at a classical radio station—involved showing up at 6:00 a.m. and basically punching buttons for someone else. But it was on-the-job experience. And the second radio job involved punching buttons and logging scripts (this meant I would write down what song played at what time).

And, because I was not making much money, I had to be creative with the money I did have. I wanted to take singing lessons at a well-known jazz club. So I worked out a deal with the owner where I would come by and clean the club once a week in exchange for jazz vocal lessons. This meant scrubbing bathrooms, dusting bookshelves and tables, and sweeping the floor. But the club's owner, who was an incredible piano player and neat lady, would often sit and talk to me while I did this, and I got to hear all kinds of cool stories about the different jazz legends she had met and worked with, including one of my favorites, Diana Krall.

It's humbling, people, but sometimes those seemingly grunt-work jobs—paid or not—can be a stepping-stone to something else.

When the Rug Gets Pulled Out from Under You

Sometimes things will happen that just don't make sense to you at the time. I was up for a big hosting job in Seattle many years ago. I flew to Seattle and interviewed for the job several times. I was certain I had the gig! My husband and I were excited about the opportunity to move home and be near our families. But at the last minute a much-loved former Seattle news anchor also auditioned for the job and they hired her. I was disappointed—this seemed like the perfect fit! But in those moments we can rest in the fact that God has things in control, and He may have something around the corner that is even better for our lives. That was the case with me. I can see now that I am exactly where I am supposed to be. But in that moment, it is okay to be disappointed. That's being human. But I believe successful people don't stay down long, they keep looking up and keep moving!

Takeaway

Imagine for a minute a beautiful tapestry. Have you ever seen someone making one? The back is a mess of multicolored threads, going every which way, zigzagging across the tapestry. It looks disorganized, it's messy, and you usually can't make out the design. But when you flip it over, it is a beautiful picture. Our lives are like the back of this tapestry when we are figuring things out, setting our goals, finding those first jobs, and listening to God. We will take zigzag twists and turns that might make life seem messy and disorganized, but one day you will see the full picture, and it will be beautiful. What we see as a mess, God sees as a masterwork in progress!

Now—and throughout your career—have a good friend you can

confide in. Someone who understands your business, whose opinion you value, and who can help you sort through any knots you encounter. I have those friends, and I try to be that friend to others. Also, try to find someone working in the same or similar field that you are. I have many friends from different industries and backgrounds, and I do seek them out for all kinds of advice. I rely on my entertainment colleagues, though, for my entertainment-industry-specific moments. They truly understand the world and the vicissitudes of my job, so they are able to offer invaluable input. I encourage you to do the same: build that support system—same industry and otherwise—around you for when those moments come, because they certainly will. But you will be ready for them.

Takeaway

1. Be persistent. That character trait is more valuable than talent or education.

2. Be creative. If you can't find a paying job, take a volunteer position or part-time position.

3. Whatever task you are given, do it as unto the Lord. He *will* bless you.

4. Find good friends to confide in and pray with you through the challenges.

5. When you're down, keep looking up and keep moving.

Over my twenty years in the agent business, I have represented hundreds of clients and negotiated thousands of contracts for talent on all the major networks and cable channels. What I've learned over the years is that in a successful negotiation, everybody has to have the same goal: to achieve a win-win for all parties. In almost any deal I do with almost any executive, it all comes down to having an honest and respectful relationship based on trust. To get there, when you negotiate, sometimes you need to stop talking, simply listen, and try to learn where the other side is coming from.

That being said, I do encourage people to take risks. Ask! Be fearless! You will never know unless you ask.

As a man of faith, I know who my Source is and that ultimately He—Jesus—is the CEO. I think whether in life or in negotiations, one must be bold. Don't take no for an answer, and never settle. Exhaust everything and always think bigger, better, and greater. Megan reminds us that this ability to negotiate effectively does not come overnight but that we learn from every experience and get a little bit better every time.

—Matthew H. Kingsley, founder and president,
3 Kings Entertainment

Eleven

Let's Negotiate!

Mastering an Intimidating Yet Essential Skill

Let us never negotiate out of fear,
but let us never fear to negotiate.

—JOHN F. KENNEDY

ALARIES. CONTRACTS. AGENTS. Negotiations. Raises. Promotions.

The minute we start to understand how the world works, we begin negotiating. My four-year-old son, Chace, is already good at it. He says, "Mama, if I eat half my peas and carrots, can I have an ice-cream sandwich?" I say, "No, you need to eat *all* your peas and carrots!" Then he will say, "If I eat half of them, can I have half an ice-cream sandwich?" Smart kid!

All joking aside, there is a lot we could probably learn from our kids—a lot about being creative and bold in our negotiations. This is a very important topic with many questions. Should we always negotiate? Should we do it ourselves, or hire an agent? And how is a believer to handle negotiations?

I don't know all the answers, but I certainly have learned a lot from the various times I've negotiated.

It's Always Negotiable

I realize not all industries have the room to negotiate. In this ever-changing economy and with companies tightening their budgets, situations may vary. But I do think it never, ever hurts to ask respectfully. This is my experience with the media world, which seems to have a bit more room for this.

I got my first radio job when I was fresh out of college, and I was offered the specific rate of ten dollars an hour. I assumed that was the pay rate and that I needed to take it. Frankly, I was just excited to have a job!

As I continued in this industry, I assumed that, for the most part, the pay I was offered was a fixed—as in cannot be changed—amount. I remember vividly a conversation with a gentleman who was offering me a radio gig. He said on the phone, "The rate is fifteen dollars an hour, nonnegotiable." And then he proceeded to talk about the other aspects of the job—the hours, the amount of air time, etc.

I remember thinking, *Okay, so the pay is nonnegotiable because he said so.* Then, not even letting me respond, he had started talking about the other details of the job. I accepted the job and worked at it for a few months. It was a great gig where I met people and made some good contacts. But after I left that particular station, I learned the person before me had been paid more. Imagine my surprise. My boss had told me the rate was nonnegotiable. Well, I learned an important lesson that day: the rate is always negotiable.

Lessons like these come with experience. I would not have traded those early radio gigs for the world—but I did need to learn how the world works and understand that negotiating and asking for more money is not a bad thing.

You Learn by Experience—and Every Experience Will Be Different

When I got my job as the morning traffic anchor for the local CBS affiliate in San Antonio, Texas, I was not hired directly by the television station, but by a media company called Metro Networks. They were supplying television stations with TV traffic reporters all over the country. So when the company pitched me to the local station in San Antonio, I was surprised at how quickly the negotiation went down. I had flown in from Nashville, taken a cab right to the station, walked into the studio, and did my on-air test. That meant doing a pretend newscast and some chatting at the anchor desk with my prospective co-anchors. Afterward, I was taken upstairs to the general manager's office.

We sat and talked for about fifteen minutes—tops! He asked me why my college major was political science and not broadcast journalism. He told me how great BELO was (the company that owned the station), asked a few questions about my current job, and told me how great living in San Antonio was (all of which ended up being true—go, Spurs!). And that was it! He shook my hand, and I walked out the door. I got into a car with the senior producer at Metro—the point person for the job—who was taking me out to dinner that night.

Within a few minutes after getting into the car, his phone rang. It was the station's general manager offering me the job. But instead of getting *me* on the phone, he proceeded to tell the producer what the offer was. The producer hung up the phone and said, "They want to hire you! They're offering a two-year contract at this amount. What do you say?" I was shocked. This was how it was going down? I had expected some paperwork to review and some time to think about it.

But as I sat there thinking about what he had said, I realized something: the number was lower than what I had been originally told. When I had first learned of the job, I was told the salary would be $36,000 the first year and $38,000 the second year. But don't get lost in the numbers. The bigger point is not the salary offered, but the *way* it was offered: in a car, in a very brief conversation in which I wasn't even involved, and with the wrong numbers. Clearly, not everything happens in an office, and you won't always have the proper paperwork in front of you or much time to read the offer and think things over!

I calmly said no to the offer and explained, "That's not the amount you originally emailed me." Stunned, the producer just looked at me. Not only was I saying no to the offer, but on top of that, I was questioning the amount.

"What do you mean? This is the offer! Do we have a deal?" He was a fast-talker trying darn hard to seal the deal right then and there. I was nervous, but I kept my wits about me. "I'm sorry, but the email said higher. I will do the job for what was originally quoted."

The producer was quiet. He then mentioned that if I would just agree to the deal, maybe we could figure out a higher amount for my second year down the road, since this was a two-year contract. I still stuck to my guns and said I needed the original amount from the beginning. He did not respond, and just drove for a while. Looking back, I think he was really shocked I did not gushingly say, "Thank you so much! You bet we have a deal!" After all, this was the number one station in the city, a large city, and I was being offered a plum assignment. The morning news was quickly becoming more visible and therefore more lucrative.

But I didn't know that. I was only twenty-four years old. All I knew was, this could be my first full-time job *and* those numbers were lower than what was originally promised. For some reason, after what I had gone through at the radio station, even if I was not going to get more, I was very sure I was at least going to hold fast to the original deal. Where that confidence came from, folks, I am not exactly sure! (Later I realized this may have been a negotiating tactic of *theirs*, because now, instead of trying to negotiate for more money, I was just trying to hold on to the original offer.)

I could tell the producer was disappointed. He had wanted me to say yes right then and there. Nevertheless, he took me out to dinner with another coworker, and we chitchatted about the city . . . but I could tell they were anxious because the deal had not been finalized.

And you know what? Looking back, I see that I was taking a major risk. There are dozens of young reporters who would love this gig. That night I called my current boss at the radio station. He had recommended me for this job, so I explained the situation to him. Most people keep their finances and salaries to themselves, but I knew I needed help and advice: *Had I made a bad move? Was I being foolish or dumb to hold out for a few thousand dollars?* My radio boss gave me some great advice that night, starting with his encouragement to definitely stick to the original offer.

He continued, "Don't ever agree to something promised in the future. These things rarely come to fruition." He then told me that when he had been promoted to director of operations for our station in Nashville, he had been promised in his contract a "raise down the road." He asked for more money before he took the position, but management said, "We don't have the ability to pay you any more right now, but if you sign this, we can talk again down the road at the midpoint of your contract." My boss signed, and halfway through his contract, they never initiated that promised conversation. When my boss brought up the original conversation they'd had, he was told that money was too tight and they would need to get to that in the *next* contract. He never got that raise, so he was adamant that I hold fast to the original deal. He knew how highly unlikely it was that the increase in pay would come later.

Then, on Monday morning, the producer emailed me. We had both found the original email, and he said he would honor those numbers. I must have had a Red Bull that day because my response was "After being to the station and assessing the situation, I am very grateful for this offer and this job. However, after learning what will be required of me, I think we need to get to at least . . . and I gave him a higher number." The producer cleared his throat and said he would get back to me. I said, "No problem."

I ended up getting just a bit more than the amount originally emailed to me. More important, I had negotiated! And I learned a valuable lesson: gather information about the job to the best of your ability, and if you think the task is worth a higher amount, ask for more. There is always room for negotiation.

Always Get a Second Opinion

Women are less likely to make a counteroffer than men are. Case in point. Betty Liu, one of the most prominent female anchors on Bloomberg Television, tells about her first big contract. When she was hired, her agent received the offer from the management of Bloomberg. When he told Betty, she was thrilled. It seemed like a great contract to her, and she accepted. Years later, when she was talking to one of the female executives involved in hiring at Bloomberg, she told Betty that management was shocked when she accepted the first offer. "No one does that! You *always* counter, Betty. Don't ever accept the first offer again."

I had a similar experience when I was hired by *Inside Edition*. When the first offer came in, it was exciting. It was six figures! I was thrilled. My agent said, "I'm really pleased with this offer. I have seen them offer much lower to starting reporters. I think we should accept it." I think the bright lights of New York City, the lure of being on a national television show, and the fact that this six-figure salary was so much more than what I was currently making clouded my judgment. Six figures in NYC is vastly different from six figures in San Antonio and most other cities in the United States. I remember my husband saying to me, "Now, I don't know the television industry, but aren't you supposed to always make a counteroffer?" So I asked my agent about this, and was told, "Well, this is an amazing offer. I think you would be hard-pressed to get a better one." I wasn't convinced.

First of all, a contract addresses more than money. These contracts include all sorts of fine points about exclusivity, the time line of negotiations, guidelines about resigning a contract, and so forth. Of course, I was pretty green on national TV contracts, but I did think we needed to negotiate some of these points. A good friend of mine had just moved to Los Angeles and was working as a producer for Dr. Phil. I called him up and said, "Hey, Mike! I just got this offer from *Inside Edition*. My agent doesn't really want to change anything, but I feel like we need to. Who is handling your contracts?"

Mike referred me to an entertainment attorney he had started working with—and God bless this guy. I emailed him and asked if he would look over my contract. He said sure, and I sent it to him. He went over it with a fine-tooth comb and marked it all up— adding notes here, crossing this out, adding that. When he faxed it back to me, it had scribbles and notes *everywhere*. I sent it over to my agent, who had wanted to change nothing. My agent's response: "Well, I mean, I guess we could ask for some of these points. But TV anchor contracts are pretty standard. I don't think they will change most of this stuff."

The entertainment attorney in LA, however, had offered another approach in his notes: "Look, if you aren't going to ask for money, then ask for another week of vacation. Ask for a clothing allowance. Ask them to cover your ticket to ride the ferry from New Jersey to New

York." I thought those were excellent suggestions. My agent and I made a list of the points that were most important to me, we let a few minor points go, and we sent the contract back to *Inside Edition*. Guess what? They agreed to the majority of my requests. Success! They were, and continue to be, very professional and pleasant to deal with.

Folks, those seemingly small points can add up to thousands of dollars! So I can't encourage you enough to always get a second opinion

I learned lessons from that first contract with *Inside Edition* that I have applied to all my jobs and contacts since then. I learned creative negotiating. Each time I was pregnant with one of my two children, *Inside Edition* has been even more gracious and accommodating. I actually installed an audio booth in my home so I could occasionally voice stories for the show while I was on maternity leave. It has been a win-win for both of us.

So, think beyond the actual dollar. And don't forget how little kids learn to negotiate; like my son with the ice cream sandwich, they are very creative! We need to take some of this creativity with us into adulthood.

You Can Be Nice

Too many people believe you can't be nice when negotiating; you need to be tough and cocky and thick-skinned and bold. Well, guess what? I think you can be tough and bold at the same time you are respectful and nice. You can be all those things and still maintain your values in the process.

Leeza Gibbons, author of the book *Fierce Optimism*, former host of the talk show *Leeza*, and winner of *Celebrity Apprentice*, wrote about this. I consider her a role model in many ways. Very few people have worked on syndicated newsmagazine shows, but Leeza worked on two shows that are very similar to mine, *Entertainment Tonight* and *Extra*. Furthermore, Leeza is one of the nicest people you will ever meet in the entertainment world. Period. Yet she was a tough negotiator.

In her book, Leeza wrote about moving from *Entertainment Tonight* to *Extra*. She and her agent were busy going back and forth with *Extra* about the details, and the communication was starting to feel angry. People were getting heated and actually slamming down phones. Leeza wasn't at all comfortable with the direction the negotiations were going, so she called a friend in the business for a second opinion. I'm paraphrasing their conversation, but it went something like this. . . .

He asked her, "Do you really want this job?" When she said, "Yes, I do. I think it's the right move for me," her friend replied, "Then don't let things get to a place where it might be hard to recover." His message was that we may need to work with—perhaps on a daily basis—the same people we might negotiate fiercely with.

So Leeza picked up the phone and called the executive in charge of the negotiations. She said, quite frankly, "Hey, I really want to work with you all. I think it will be a great fit, and I don't want to lose sight of that. Can we find some common ground here and get to a place that feels good for both of us?" The executive responded well to this, and they worked out a deal. After she started at *Extra*, when Leeza saw that executive in the hall, she felt good about how she had handled the negotiations. She had been tough but pleasant, and that was important to her. At the end of the day, the tone of the discussion was more important to her than some of the finer points of the contract. And her pleasantness paid off.

And that's how I conduct my negotiations. I remain pleasant even as I stand firm. Remember how I successfully negotiated some extra items into my first national TV contract? Well fast-forward several years later: when I wanted to move from full-time to part-time, *Inside*

Edition was very accommodating and supportive. The discussion of the details and the actual transition itself always remained pleasant, and their support continues. When I got my book deal, my bosses at *Inside Edition* were some of the first people I told, and their advice and support have been significant. I believe this kind of working relationship comes back to how you handle yourself in important moments such as during contract negotiation.

Know When to Stop

I can definitely testify to the importance of this guideline!

When I was negotiating my second year with *Thursday Night Football*, I was hoping for a nice bump in my salary. When the offer came in at the exact same amount as the first year, I was very disappointed. Yes, the job was incredible, but it was a *ton* of work. I felt I was paid way too little for the work required. So I pushed back and asked for more. My boss responded by saying the amount he had offered was the amount he had budgeted for the job, so he would have to go back to corporate to request more money—and that process might take a while.

Right away I thought this was a negotiating tactic. So I said, "All right. I'll wait for your good news."

And I waited. And waited. And waited. Weeks started going by, and I had not heard back. I asked my dad what he thought, and he told me to sit tight. I asked my hubby, and he told me to sit tight. But I was getting anxious. In addition to waiting on that contract, I was pregnant with our second child—and my boss knew this. I was due about six weeks before the first *Thursday Night Football* game. I figured that was still pretty good timing: I would get a C-section (as I had with my first baby) and therefore schedule the birth. All set, right? I had assured my boss all would be fine.

But as I was waiting for him to get back to me, I started wondering if this was the best situation to be in while I was pregnant. I went to a dear family friend who had run her own business in New York City. I needed to hear from someone who had hired and fired people. I explained my situation, and I'll never forget what Trish said to me: "Well, Megan, I will be honest. If I were your employer and you were holding out for more money and also pregnant, I would be actively looking for your replacement. Several weeks have gone by, you have not heard back, and you have some extra variables going on with the situation." And then she asked me what Leeza's friend had asked her: "Do you really want this job?"

"Yes! It's the NFL! I love it!"

"And do you like your boss?"

"Very much," I responded.

"Then I think it's up to you to get the conversation moving again."

The next day I called my boss and told him I wanted to figure this out. I explained that I love the job and the people I work with, so I wanted to sign a contract. I proceeded to ask him for less than I had originally requested, but an amount that was still a slight raise. He said, "Megan, this is interesting timing. Corporate literally just told me we need to keep our budgets tight. So I can't give you what you originally asked for, but how about this?" I said, "Yes! We have a deal!"

When I hung up the phone, I felt really good about both my decision and that conversation. I had gotten a slight bump in pay, but I had maintained my relationship with my boss, whom I really respect and like. It was a win-win. It also looked like I had helped him out by getting the deal wrapped up. In that situation, knowing when to stop was the right move for me. I was at peace.

Not every negotiation will be perfectly peaceful or pleasant, though. That is simply the reality we live in, but we can control our own response to situations however unpleasantly they may be going.

The Bible says, "If it is possible, as far as it depends on you, live at peace with everyone" (Romans 12:18 NIV). Let me make this very clear: being a peaceful person does *not* mean being weak or a pushover. Not at all! Instead, I believe there is a peaceful way to be tough and bold in your negotiations and still feel good about them at the end of the day.

I wouldn't be honest if I didn't say I felt I deserved more than I negotiated for in season 2, but the factors involved in reaching a settlement don't always lead to that. I needed to negotiate and then settle in light of what I had going on in my personal life. I did that, we had reached a deal, and I felt good about it. And the most successful negotiation is truly when both sides feel successful. Legendary sports agent Leigh Steinberg, on whom the movie *Jerry Maguire* was based, said this: "It's learning how to negotiate to keep both sides happy—whether it's for a multimillion-dollar contract or just which show to watch on TV that determines the quality and enjoyment of our lives."

The Walk-Away Method

Another strategy in negotiating is walking away. This is not my style, but recently I inadvertently used this strategy, and it ended up working to my advantage.

An organization approached me about hosting a weekend event for them and emailed the initial offer. I had just had my second baby, Catcher, so I forwarded the email to my publicist, and she took over. I was super busy with the new baby and going back to work for both *Football* and *Inside Edition*, so my publicist and I decided to email them back and ask for a much higher amount. A day later the organization emailed back and said they wished they had that kind of a budget, but they simply didn't. They offered a slightly higher day rate than they originally offered, but I still did not think it was high enough.

I really enjoy emceeing events and probably would have taken the second offer a year earlier, but at that point I just felt too busy. We emailed back our thanks, but declined the invitation. They did not email back for several days, so I thought the matter was closed. About a week later the organization emailed my publicist offering triple what the first offer was. I was surprised they were willing to offer me so much money! I discussed the opportunity with my family: we all agreed it was a great offer and I should emcee the event.

I tell this story because I literally walked away from the second offer. I said no and really meant it. But then they came back with a much higher number than I'd imagined. They may have thought my response was just a negotiating ploy, but I truly was too busy with my family. Regardless, it revealed they had way more of a budget than they'd originally stated.

If I had really wanted that job, I wouldn't have said no so many times. In fact, as I stated earlier, I would have probably taken the second offer. But look what happened when I walked away! I learned from this experience.

But if you use this tactic when negotiating a job you really want, beware! It can be an effective strategy, but it's risky. You need to be very sure you are okay with that opportunity never coming back.

Agent or No Agent?

Sometimes I have used an agent, and sometimes I haven't. In the above scenario, I asked my publicist to help me negotiate. But you may recall that when I was hired in San Antonio, I didn't have an agent. I see advantages and disadvantages to both choices.

Having an agent can mean someone has your back, and that can be very nice. It can also be easier to let an agent handle the nuts-and-bolts conversations. And having your agent represent you and negotiate for you can be beneficial if you don't have the confidence to discuss money and what your services are worth. But it is absolutely essential that you share a vision and a genuine camaraderie with your agent. He or she needs to have your own best interest at heart, and some agents do not. Some just want their clients to climb the ladder regardless of whether or not a specific move is a good fit now and/or a valuable stepping-stone. I did not always see eye to eye with my first agent, and I ended up letting her go. I was better off alone for a while. When I did eventually pursue a new agent, I made sure our personalities and communication skills were compatible.

The primary benefit of my negotiating my first San Antonio TV contract and later the *Thursday Night Football* contract all by myself was exactly that: I did it all myself. I learned how to talk money, how to stand up for myself, how to ask for what I wanted, and how to communicate all this with diplomacy and humility. Yes, we can be bold and confident during negotiations, but I knew I also wanted to stay positive and classy throughout the process. My father has always said, "You really learn who a person is when you play competitive sports with them." The same can be said of negotiating. Once you start talking money and contracts, the way each person handles the conversations says a lot about their character.

Most television personalities, sports stars, and actors do have agents. Having someone else negotiate one's contracts is a pretty standard practice in the entertainment industry. As a result, there are many very qualified agents who know the business inside and out and have great contacts. But every now and then you will hear of someone who still negotiates his or her own contracts. Such was the case with Jim Zorn.

Zorn was the quarterback for the Seattle Seahawks from 1976 to

1984. He went on to play for the Green Bay Packers and Tampa Bay Buccaneers. After retiring from play, he became head coach of the Washington Redskins. He was known for not using an agent when he played for the Seahawks. At the time, the Nordstrom family, of the famed department store chain, owned the team, and they spoke of the pleasant, straightforward negotiations they conducted with Zorn. He must have done just fine because he stayed as starting quarterback with the Hawks for seven years. Zorn is an unusual example, but it worked for him—he was successful. Clearly, negotiating for oneself can be done.

Sometimes Patience Is Required

Sometimes negotiations and getting to the job will try your patience. My friend Matthew Kingsley, a talent agent, shares this story:

> *Early in my career, I had just signed this incredibly talented sports anchor in a Midwest city. Unfortunately, once his contract was up, it was not renewed and he was unemployed for the first time in his career. Things became very difficult for him, and he was forced to sell cars and paint houses—whatever it took to take care of his family. During this transitional period, I was able to get him many interviews throughout the country in a few local markets and even with a national network, but nothing worked out. Eighteen months went by; still no job. He became discouraged. Then one day I received a call from a friend at CNN. He said, "Your client's luck is about to change. CNN is getting ready to launch their sister network, HLN, and we want to hire your client to be the morning sports anchor for our new national show." I immediately called my client with the good news and he burst into tears. It was then an easy*

*negotiation for both sides because both wanted to be in busi-
ness with the other. My client had been patient and waited for
the right opportunity.*

I appreciate this story because it's a good reminder that sometimes
we need to be patient—at times, more patient than we ever imagined.
But if we trust in the Lord and continue to work hard and develop the
right relationships, good things will come. This client could have fired
Matthew after a few months of no work coming in. But the two of
them must have developed a solid relationship of trust because they
both waited it out, and eventually the perfect job opened up. The negotiation that resulted was positive and exciting for both sides. Another win-win.

And a Word to the Ladies . . .

Mika Brzezinski, one of the morning anchors on MSNBC's program
Morning Joe, wrote *Knowing Your Value,* a fantastic book about negotiations and her journey to understanding her value in the business and
television worlds. She believes it is imperative that we women know
our worth in the world, and referring to her own experiences in television, Mika encourages women to be strong and bold in their contract
and salary negotiations. She states, "Knowing the fair-market value of
our contributions at work is a critically important piece of knowledge
for today and tomorrow's professional woman." How do we do this?
How do we determine the value of our work? We do some research.
We ask around. We work hard, and when it comes time to negotiate,
we apply the principles listed above.

Women don't tend to talk much about negotiating salary, which is
why this chapter needed to be in this book. I don't pretend to know all
the answers, but I hope my stories and experiences encourage you to

be a little bit bolder during your next contract or job negotiation. I firmly believe that skillful negotiating is crucial to providing for our families.

One final thought: work on sharpening your negotiating skills. Take a class at a local community college, find a workshop in negotiating, or attend a two-day Karrass Seminar on negotiating (www. karass.com). (I have been wanting to sign up for one myself!) And anyone can read a book on the topic. In addition to Mika Brzezinski's *Knowing Your Value*, my favorites include *The Art of the Deal* by Donald Trump, *The Confidence Code: The Science and Art of Self-Assurance— What Women Should Know* by Katty Kay and Claire Shipman, and *Lean In: Women, Work, and the Will to Lead* by Sheryl Sandberg. Choose one of these or another of the many more books out there. Read up and perfect the skill of negotiation. From buying a car to negotiating that first work contract to hammering out the details of starting your own business to determining how much of our vegetables we need to eat before we can have an ice-cream sandwich, we are *always* negotiating!

Takeaway

1. Everything is negotiable, so be bold and creative in the fine print of a contract.

2. Always get a second opinion.

3. The ultimate success is when both parties are happy.

4. Determine if you want to do the negotiating yourself or get an agent or lawyer to do it on your behalf. Both approaches can be beneficial.

5. The art and skill of negotiating can help you better provide for yourself and your loved ones. When pregnancies come or health issues strike, learning how to negotiate may help you figure out child care, flexible hours, or a bonus based on productivity.

*W*aiting for sex until marriage is one of the greatest, most profound, and most life-changing decisions you can make. Too often in our fast-paced and sex-crazed culture, even we Christians overlook the decisions we make in our love lives as inconsequential to the blessings we're expecting God to work in our lives overall. However, nothing could be further from the truth. The decisions we make privately are the very decisions that determine the quality of the life we experience publicly. And waiting until marriage for sex is a key decision that can unlock unprecedented success and joy in our lives. Megan's courage to share this aspect of her story will challenge you, inspire you, and maybe even help save your life.

—DeVon Franklin, president/CEO of Franklin Entertainment and *New York Times* bestselling author of *The Wait*

Twelve

Sleep Your Way to the Top

Let the Uncool Be What's Cool

Don't let anyone look down on you because you are young, but set an example for the believers in speech, in conduct, in love, in faith and in purity.

1 TIMOTHY 4:12 NIV

So WHY WOULD I INCLUDE A CHAPTER on abstinence in a book about succeeding at work? The chapter title answers that question, at least in part. Many people think the concept of abstinence is out of place and old-fashioned. I get it; believe me. That idea is reinforced all the time in my industry. But I'm addressing abstinence because this personal choice has become a theme in my professional life. And instead of abstinence hindering my career advancement in any way, I can confidently say the opposite is true. Even though our culture encourages otherwise, I have thrived with my choice. But I realize I am not the norm and the conversation is a rare one.

Paradigm Shift

Let's face it: We live in a sex-crazed world. We are bombarded with sex everywhere we look. It's in our schools, it's in our magazines, it's on our televisions, computers, and phones. I am often disappointed in Hollywood's portrayal of love. Movies and television make it seem like people should participate in sex as easily and as often as they brush their teeth!

Sadly, entertainment does little to encourage abstinence. Phone apps like Tinder can connect you to people looking for a quick hookup—no strings attached. As a culture, we are told there are no rules; you can do whatever you want, whenever you want. And along the way, never give any regard to the consequences or the wake of destruction you might leave in your path.

Also fueling this sexual freedom is our culture's message that one's self-esteem is based on how much sex a person can experience and how many men or women a person can conquer. Further, if you are a virgin or are saving yourself for marriage, you are considered old-fashioned and out of touch. Young people are faced with an incredible amount of pressure to jump into a relationship physically—and they are encountering this pressure at younger ages all the time.

Perhaps, not surprising in this culture of ours, one consequence of cheapening sex is the devaluing of marriage. We live in a world where marriage is too often looked at not as a lifetime commitment but as a contract one can always opt out of. With this attitude permeating our culture, we shouldn't be surprised by the number of broken homes and broken lives.

Clearly, in our Tinder culture, abstinence requires a huge paradigm shift. Before people make that shift, they may look at my decision to wait and be confused or amused. But I believe there are more people out there who are still weighing the decision. And they are offered very little encouragement or role models from the abstinence side.

In a world of "I want what I want whenever I want it," the selflessness that comes with abstinence does not make much sense. But this choice is not just about saying no to yourself for a season. Abstinence is about putting the other person above yourself and saying they are worth the wait. You forgo the instant gratification of your own personal desires so you can create an even better and lasting future, and attempt to avoid pain and hurt along the way.

I cringe at how lightly the world treats sex. God created us such complex and sensitive human beings. We are not just our bodies, and sex is not just a flesh-to-flesh connection. I think today's society cheapens sex because it doesn't understand what God intended sex to be: an extremely intimate, spiritual act that bonds you with someone's heart, soul, mind, and emotions. I waited because I wanted to share that act with only one person.

As always, God's commands are for our good. In 1 Thessalonians 4:3, Paul wrote, "It is God's will that you should be sanctified: that you should avoid sexual immorality" (NIV). Paul addressed this same topic in his letter to the people of Corinth: "Flee from sexual immorality. All other sins a person commits are outside the body, but whoever sins sexually, sins against their own body" (1 Corinthians 6:18 NIV). The Bible tells us to "Above all else, guard your heart" (Proverbs 4:23 NIV). We risk guarding our hearts when we choose to have sex before marriage.

Whoa!

My own personal decision to abstain became public for a variety of reasons. While walking the streets of Manhattan one day, my phone rang. Lynette, my pastor's wife in New York, was calling. She told me she had just spoken with a friend who was the publisher of a women's magazine. They were planning an issue on sex and marriage, and they wanted to do a cover story on a young female who was prominent in the entertainment or media world and who had practiced abstinence before she'd gotten married. Lynette said to me, "She's been asking around, and she can't find anyone! I told her I knew someone, but I wasn't sure she'd be interested in going public about this."

That someone was me—and Lynette was right; as she'd guessed, I wasn't so sure I wanted to be in the spotlight for this reason.

After all, I had been hoping to be able to just blend into the working world and simply do my job. But I sensed God was nudging me to showcase my faith more boldly. Colossians 1:10 came to mind: "The way you live will always honor and please the Lord, and your lives will produce every kind of good fruit. All the while, you will grow as you learn to know God better and better."

I told Lynette I would think about it and get back to her. That night I told my husband about this opportunity and asked him what he thought. After all, he was one-half of the scenario. Going public with my story would mean going public with his, too. My husband had already had sex before he came to faith, but he decided to abstain until we got married (this is sometimes called "second virginity"). Brian thought about it for a moment and then said, "We say we always want to honor God in whatever we do. I never thought it would be this way, but why not?"

We both agreed that these days not just teens, but everyone, is facing an incredible amount of pressure to jump into bed before marriage. Movies, television, and advertising all portray premarital sex as normal. Abstinence isn't a popular topic, and no one seems to be talking about it. If they do talk about it, it seems to be met with a lot of sarcasm and shock. If sharing our story would make it "cool" to follow our path, and help people realize abstinence is an option, then our going public about our experience would be worth it.

So I wrote an article for the magazine. I hoped it might inspire a few people, but I never expected a big response.

Print, Television, and the Internet

At *Inside Edition*, my fellow reporters and I often do side projects. For example, Lisa Guerrero paints mosaics and sometimes takes bit parts in movies. Steve Kamer, the voice of our show, does voice-overs on everything from NASH-FM to movie trailers. When any of the on-air talent gets a big gig, we are supposed to let our boss know about it. So when the magazine was published with me on the cover, I put a copy on my boss's desk with a Post-it note that said, "Hey, boss! Wanted to let you know I wrote an article about my marriage for this magazine. Just a heads-up! Thanks!"

I didn't expect to hear from him when I left for the evening. But that night my boss emailed me. He said, "Megan, I am so glad you gave me this magazine. Not only is it a great article, but I think it's very profound. I would like to do a story on the show about you and your husband and your decision to wait. Would you be interested?"

I looked up from my computer and called to my husband, "Oh, Bri-an . . ." and shared the email. God bless that man! His response remained the same: "If it helps one person, it's worth it." So my husband and I sat down for an interview with Deborah Norville, the host of *Inside Edition*, and the show ran my story. It was odd being on the other end of the interview for a change! Soon after, Fox News called and asked if they could put the story on their website—and I learned later that it was the number three trending story on FoxNews.com for that entire day.

I do not share this to brag, but because it indicates that people are interested in the conversation. People want to talk about it, and they have many questions. And I want single people to know they are not alone in choosing purity and that it isn't weird to decide to wait until marriage to have sex. This choice worked for me, and it can work for them and for you.

When Seattle Seahawks star quarterback Russell Wilson announced he and pop singer Ciara were waiting until marriage to have sex, the world responded with ridicule, amusement, and only occasional admiration. Wilson was being interviewed at Rock Church in San Diego by head pastor Miles McPherson, a former NFL Chargers player. When the story was picked up by the media, many people in the sports and entertainment worlds ridiculed Wilson. Others just dismissed him as old-fashioned and odd.

Yet I think many people were struck by how unselfish and unusual Wilson's decision was. By waiting, he was showing that he loves and respects Ciara. During the interview he said, "I asked her 'What would you do if we took all that other stuff off the table and did it Jesus' way, no sex?'"*

In our sex-obsessed pop culture, Wilson's decision stood out and attracted attention. As I sat in my cubicle at the *Inside Edition* offices and reported the story, I was smiling and silently cheering him on. I think Russell and Ciara are to be admired for their choice. I made the same one—and, as I've said, you can, too. And as my husband, Brian, did, regardless of your past experiences, you can always make the decision now to wait for your future spouse.

Why I Decided to Wait for Marriage

Early on in my life, I determined to approach marriage in the best way I could. One night two graduates who were dating—and waiting—

---

* www.christianpost.com/news/seattle-seahawks-qb-russell-wilson-tells-rock-church-he
-and-ciara-are-dating-jesus-way-abstaining-from-sex-141231/

came to my high school to talk to us about the pros and cons of abstinence. What unfolded was an honest, candid conversation about marriage and sex, and it was an important moment for me. They talked about how little in our world is sacred anymore, and they told us how fun the anticipation of sex can be. They were looking forward to their life together and didn't want to rush those moments. They also wanted to be sure the other was "the one."

I remember some people in the room feeling and looking embarrassed. It was a deeply personal topic these two were discussing—with high school students! But I am so grateful they did. And I thought of them when I was asked to share my abstinence story . . . on national television! They had stepped out of their comfort zone to speak to us that night in high school. It was uncomfortable, but it had been so valuable and insightful. I wanted to do the same with my story. Someone needed to do it now, and I felt God prompting me.

I had another profound insight when I was a junior in high school. My friends and I were having a discussion when I realized that every guy friend of mine was someone's future husband. Likewise, each of their girlfriends was someone's future wife. I suddenly had a new outlook on dating. Instead of simply having fun and acting selfishly, only caring about myself and what I wanted, I became conscious of how I was treating others, realizing they were someone's potential spouse. Instead of trying to "get" whatever we could, we started thinking of "saving" what we could for our future spouses. When you start looking at it from a difference perspective, it really does change your mind-set.

But Is Abstinence Realistic?

Teenagers, coworkers, and peers ask me all the time, "Was abstinence difficult for you? How did you do it?" I think a few things helped me stay focused on my goal.

First, I stayed busy. I focused on pursuing my career. I took on extra jobs in radio and television. I volunteered, traveled the country, cultivated hobbies, and stayed involved in church. I met all kinds of wonderful, diverse, and like-minded people. I stayed busy and kept setting goals for myself. I sincerely believe one of the keys to my abstinence success was this: I was too busy chasing my dreams to get in trouble with boys. The verse 1 Thessalonians 4:4 says, "Each of you should learn to control your own body in a way that is holy and honorable (NIV)." I believe that, by staying busy and involved, I trained my body and my heart to wait.

Then, later in my life, I found a man who respected me and my decision. He believed he should wait, too. Brian and I dated for five years, and during that time he never pressured me to do anything I did not want to do. We decided on our boundaries, and we stuck to them. Accountability was crucial, so we held each other accountable. That meant sometimes I was the strong one—heading home early or planning dates away from secluded spots—and sometimes Brian was. Both of us needed to be steadfast in our commitment.

Supermodel Adriana Lima—who also waited until marriage—put it this way: guys "have to respect that this is my choice. If there's no respect, that means they don't want me."* Be bold! Dare to be different! Be proud of who you are and what you have to offer! Don't rush into anything physical just because your peers are. Think for yourself. Value yourself and all you have to offer. In doing this, it is never too early to starting preparing for your future marriage.

+ Ladies and Gentlemen, I encourage you to respect yourselves and treat your bodies like temples. Choose modesty along with abstinence. Be hard to get. Get to know each other for your minds and souls.

---

* http://m.huffpost.com/us/entry/3895345.

✦ Seek a partner who believes in you and your dreams, who will support you in all areas of your life, someone who will be your best friend and biggest cheerleader. Look beyond the physical because when the going gets tough, you want a teammate who will grab your hand and pray with you.

Saving yourself for marriage is not just about sex. It represents a bigger decision, a decision to place a high value on your own worth and a commitment to God to be a great spouse and, later, a great parent. Saving yourself is just one aspect of it.

An Important Word

I realize not everyone has the opportunity to do it this way. If you are reading this and did not wait or didn't have the option to, know there is always a chance for a fresh start. God will redeem the past. He promises that in His Word (see Psalm 103:2–4). *Please hear these words*: Regardless of what choice you make on this subject, you are beautiful, loved, and just as precious to God as the couples who waited. This chapter is meant to offer encouragement and another perspective, but never to judge.

And if you have faced difficult circumstances surrounding sex, I recommend seeking professional help. Many trained counselors have expertise in healing sexual wounds. Their wisdom and guidance can make a life-changing difference for you.

Let me offer a word of hope and reassurance if you were never given the choice to wait, if—to be specific—you have been in a sexually abusive situation. That abuse was *not* your fault. Believe that—and also believe you can still make the decision to wait. Waiting is a decision of the heart as much as one of the body. Don't let anyone ever shame you or judge you for what happened *to* you in your past. Your decision to wait is and always will be *your* decision, and no one else's. Turn to God for renewal, comfort, healing, peace, and hope.

Already Married?

Whether we chose to wait or didn't, once we are married, we all can benefit from this same piece of advice: Surround yourselves with a community of encouragement and that ancient wisdom: "Walk with the wise and become wise, for a companion of fools suffers harm" (Proverbs 13:20 NIV).

When my husband and I were standing at the altar with our large bridal party, our pastor looked at all our bridesmaids and groomsmen and encouraged them to not just stand with us on our wedding day, but for the rest of our lives—to encourage us in our marriage as long as we lived.

Can you imagine if every bridesmaid and groomsman in every wedding took that charge seriously? What if they really did reach out and encourage the bride and groom, not just on the wedding day, but through the years? Maybe we would have a few more lasting marriages. I have been a bridesmaid in many weddings, and I try to keep in touch with those brides and grooms and see how they are doing when the honeymoon wears off. I know how important and impactful it is to support one another's marriages.

Before we were married, Brian and I knew we needed to work on any issues we might have, so we went through premarital counseling. And that counseling didn't stop for us once we got married. My husband and I still attend a marriage Sunday school class, and we regularly check in with a marriage counselor or pastor. We both believe every marriage needs a checkup once in a while. We are all victims of the Fall; there is no way around it. Perhaps those checkups are especially important for us because Brian comes from a broken home. But in a way I think his experience has made our marriage even stronger. It has forced us—in a good way—to have some conversations we might not have had otherwise. We have had to dive in and talk about what it will take for us to make it as a couple; we have had to be intentional about protecting our marriage. Brian understands firsthand how important it is *not* to have an exit strategy. Life happens and sometimes families don't stay together, but you have a heck of a better chance if you do all you can to prepare for what marriage and family involves. Trust me: abstinence may be one way you can prepare that solid foundation for your marriage, your family, and your home, as well as be more ready for life's inevitable storms.

Takeaway

I included this chapter because a personal decision I made became a national story that impacted my career. I am writing about it because if you find yourself living out your faith in the spotlight, a personal decision you make may become more visible than you ever anticipated or desired. But if we want to follow God with all our heart, all our soul, and all our mind (Matthew 22:37 NIV), then we need to think about what this means exactly and what it might require of us.

1. It's absolutely, definitely, unquestionably okay to wait to have sex until you are married. That plan worked for me; it can work for you!

2. Marriage is tough. Saving sex for marriage is one more way to prepare you and fortify your marriage.

3. Seek like-minded friends who share your values and can support you as you live out your decision.

4. Don't ever let anyone make you feel bad about your choices.

5. There is always a chance for a fresh start—God can make all things new.

6. Your personal choices may become a testimony of your faith. I never thought my personal choice to wait would be on public display, but because it is, I can encourage others.

*Y*es, I competed onstage in a swimsuit at Miss America. And, yes, today I work in television as a political commentator. And though I'm not talking on TV in a bikini (thank goodness!), there is still a whole lot of judgment based on looks. So how are my mission and my vocation not paradoxical?

We can celebrate female beauty without overly sexualizing women. We can wear beautiful clothing and dresses on TV without wearing skirts so short that, when we are seated in a chair, leave little to the imagination. A certain beauty and incredible internal strength come from being able to embrace the uniqueness of being a woman, with all that has to offer, including physical beauty). Yet we must constantly work against stereotypes, not backing down in the face of ignorance, and not conforming to the world's view that a woman can only be smart or beautiful, but not both. This chapter delves into this discussion, and I believe it will empower women to embrace who God created them to be.

Young women need excellent role models, and Megan is one of those. I'm blessed to call her my friend. She understands—as I do—that we can help the next generation of young women develop a sense of self-worth by being the kind of self-accepting, body-positive role models that they need.

—Kirsten Haglund-Smith, Miss America 2008

Thirteen

Redefining Beauty

Healthy Body Image in a Photoshopped World

Beauty begins the moment you decide to be yourself.

—COCO CHANEL

L IVING OUT YOUR FAITH oftentimes means simply being comfortable in your own skin. But some of us in the beauty-obsessed media world can find it pretty challenging to be content with what we look like. Even though we believe God created us in all shapes and sizes and there is beauty in diversity and variety, the world pushes back and says we need to meet its standards of beauty and physical perfection if we are to fit in. My career has brought me to an interesting place: living out my faith at work requires me to meet some of the world's standards.

Mention the words *sex, modesty, feminism,* and *beauty,* and you will get a million different viewpoints. It's no secret American marketing is all about appearance and sexuality. Flip through almost any magazine or online article, and you'll see that ads rely on images of handsome men and beautiful, sometimes barely dressed women to sell everything from razors to race cars. No wonder statistics tell us that 70 percent of all young women have some type of body-image disorder. In the faith community, everyone has a different idea of what's okay and what isn't in terms of how you dress. Take Ayesha Curry . . .

A Modest Situation

Ayesha Curry, wife of Golden State Warriors basketball star Stephen Curry, recently tweeted: "Everyone's into barely wearing clothes these days, huh? Not my style. I like to keep the good stuff covered up for the one who matters," she wrote. She received a dramatic reaction on Twitter, both positive and negative. Some praised her thoughts while others disagreed.

One response even said, "Sounds as if Ayesha Curry thinks her body/other women's bodies are like consumer goods marketed exclusively for use by men, or something." I found this fascinating. Here Ayesha was simply suggesting that people should cover up a little more, yet she was accused of viewing her body as consumer goods. I don't think that's what she meant at all. But it just illustrates how vocal our culture is about something so personal.

God created us to have ideas, and He allows us to make choices. We live in a country where we are free to dress and wear what we please. We are incredibly blessed. Women in Middle Eastern countries are forced to cover up their bodies completely. This may be the free choice of some, but it isn't for others. We should appreciate and value our freedom to dress however we want. But with that freedom comes choice.

Whether we like it or not, our image plays a role in how people perceive us. This is so true in my business. I am not complaining, because I signed up for this. I knew going in that TV is image-based and full of beautiful people. I can't be a crybaby, whine, and wish it were different. But I can carefully decide what I want my appearance to be and how much effort I want to put into establishing and maintaining my image.

You need to make this decision as well. I want to encourage you to take control of your image and offer you tips and ideas to decide well and glorify God. Perhaps you have never thought about how your choice of clothes can reflect your values and, therefore, your faith. But it's true: the choices we make say a lot about what's important to us. And, no matter how we were raised, what climate we live in, what sports or dance activities we participate in, our attire reflects our values.

I don't think there is a one-size-fits-all policy when it comes to how we dress. What you decide is going to be different from that of someone else, based on—among other factors—your work environment, body type, age, taste, and even budget. This is a complicated topic to address because we have individual comfort levels, different interpretations of the word *modesty*, and unique life situations. When deciding what clothes to buy and wear, I think about what image I want to project to the world. My decision will be different from yours—and that is a beautiful thing!

For me, establishing my image came down to valuing my body, treating it with care and respect, and deciding what "honoring God with my *whole* self" means to me. Here are some of my thoughts:

The Wrong Fit

Have you ever worn something that just didn't fit right and made you feel uncomfortable all day long? Maybe it was a shirt or a dress. I've had those moments. And because I have to worry about so many things with my job—showing up on time, asking the right questions, delivering an on-air news story with high energy, accuracy, and enthusiasm—the last thing I want to worry about is my clothes. So early on I started dressing for comfort. Now I have one fewer thing to worry about and one more source of confidence.

How will you make this choice for yourself? You could start by asking this question: Is there a difference between dressing beautifully and dressing for attention? For example, I would wear a beautiful dress that fit my body well and complemented my skin tone but did not show too much skin, and I would not wear a dress with a thigh-high slit and a deep V in the front that revealed a lot of cleavage. I personally decided I want people to think I look nice and beautiful, but not see too much of my body. Again, this is my personal choice. You need to decide what's okay for you.

What Is Your Intention?

Other questions to ask yourself when deciding how to dress are: What is my intention? Who am I dressing for? Would I wear a dress showing off cleavage just for myself or my girlfriends? Or am I wearing it for a reaction from men? My family? My friends? Answering these questions really helps me sort out my choices. I want to dress for me and my standards. Ultimately, those standards are to glorify God with my clothing choices.

I'm not saying it's easy to figure out. Every person is different. Take my good friend Charlotte Oldbury, for example. Charlotte is a bodybuilder and fitness competitor. The fitness contests she participates in require her to walk the stage and flex her muscles while wearing a pretty revealing bikini. She is in an environment where she is being judged on her muscle tone, strength, fitness level, and physique. She is also a person of faith and a happily married mother of three.

How does she reconcile everything? Charlotte says that just as an Olympic swimmer wears a Speedo to compete in races but board shorts to the beach, she wears a bikini to compete and more conservative clothing in her everyday life. Guided by her faith, she has decided this is her comfort level. There are probably plenty of people who would disagree, but others would support her decision. Again, Charlotte prayerfully figured out what was right for her.

I believe the Bible does give us some general guidelines but no exact rules for how to dress. The Bible teaches us "your bodies are temples of the Holy Spirit, who is in you, whom you have received from God" (1 Corinthians 6:19 NIV). I take this to mean that whenever people look at Megan Alexander, they are not only seeing Megan, the TV host, author, wife, and mother, they are also seeing Megan, child of God. This simple perspective causes me to reflect on who I am and what image I am projecting. If God lives in me, He will then affect my clothing choices. I will decide what to wear based on what brings Him glory and honor.

Your Own Style

The clothes we choose are just one part of the discussion, and even though I'm not crazy about it, I realize my physical appearance matters in my industry. What I choose to wear is just one factor contributing to my image. I need to look neat, put together, physically fit, and even, at times, glamorous. Still, my personal opinion is that our culture places way too much emphasis on attractiveness. Since I work in a very beauty-driven business, I have to think about it more often than not.

When I cover the Met Gala in New York City, for example, I often ask the celebrities, "How long did it take you to get ready tonight? What was your beauty routine?" They almost always answer with something like "Oh, we started this morning! It's a six-hour process of skin, hair, makeup, nails, dress fitting, jewelry," etc. Do I think this is a bit ridiculous? *Yes!* Listen, I am one of those people who gets antsy when I've been at the hair salon for more than an hour. I hate sitting still—and I don't like people tugging or pulling on my hair or skin for very long.

Since my face and my body are part of my calling card, I try to go to the gym three or four times a week, I watch what I eat, and I take care of myself to the best of my ability. This is easier said than done because I love Mexican food, chocolate, and french fries! In moderation, all of these things are fine. But again, because God made me with more of an hourglass figure, I can't indulge every day in my favorite things and skip the gym. Cardio has always been a key component to my staying in shape. I also feel better when I exercise. I love group fitness classes and high-energy music. The hour passes quickly, and through cardio, I relieve stress and stay in shape.

But I'll be honest; it's hard to keep being in shape a healthy goal when we are constantly bombarded with images of super-skinny girls on magazine covers in the grocery store or on the runways. Something that has helped is for me to find my style and stick with it. And I have to remember that those Photoshopped girls do not define style for me. I have to do that for myself.

Defining Your Own Style

Some people change their style quite drastically throughout their careers, while others decide on a look and stick with it. Others—actors and models among them—are told what their look should be. But I was never really advised or told what my style needed to be. I learned to figure out my style pretty quickly as I moved from one job to the next. When I first got to NYC to work for *Inside Edition*, they wanted to do a headshot. So when I arrived for my photo shoot, one of the first things *Inside Edition* did was send me to the makeup and hair stylist for a "touchup" even though I already had on my own makeup on. In the television industry, when you are getting a headshot for work, the promotions department or those in charge of putting together billboards and promotional materials will usually look you over and make minor adjustments—or at times even ask you to make more drastic changes—depending on how they evaluate you. Often the first question the stylist asks is "What is your style? How do you like your makeup and your look?" I quickly learned that I am a "natural, browns, peaches-and-cream girl," which means I like natural makeup colors on my face.

Regardless of my outfit, I know that brown eye shadow and eyeliner, peach blush, bronzers, and a soft golden-peach lip gloss will look good on my skin tone and work with pretty much any outfit. I have a nice mix of these colors in my makeup bag. I use some expensive products, like Smashbox or Dior foundation, but you will also find several Wet n Wild lip glosses in my bag. They cost ninety-nine cents and I love them! They are frequently on my lips for *Inside Edition*.

But sometimes the makeup artist will *not* ask what my style is and instead just get to work. When I started appearing on CNN's program *Showbiz Tonight*, and I walked into the makeup room full of makeup artists who were usually so busy with the multitude of CNN shows that they did not always have time to ask about my look. They just glanced at us me and, based on what they thought would look good, started picking up makeup brushes and going to town. After wearing bright-red lipstick and very thick black eyeliner on CNN one night, I learned to speak up. The next time I sat in the makeup chair, I said, "Hi there! I am a natural girl. I don't like anything too bold or crazy. Brown and peach colors work best for me. Thanks for understanding!" Nine times out of ten the stylist will say, "Thanks for mentioning that," and make sure I am okay with all the colors she is using. I walk away feeling good about the process, feeling like myself, and ready to focus on the assignment. I feel like Megan Alexander, not someone else. It's what makes me unique.

I frequently turn down the professional makeup artist at work. Why? Because although occasionally it's fun to have my makeup done for a big event or party, I usually find what they put on me doesn't make me feel like myself. I hosted an event recently for another net-work, and the makeup artist put these huge false eyelashes on me. I felt silly! It was just not me. It's fine if Beyoncé or Katy Perry wants to wear those, but I didn't feel right. So I went to the bathroom and took them off. Knowing what you like and what looks good on you—this is part of defining your own style.

Embracing How God Made You

Every now and then, though, people won't want you to define your own style. They will want to change you. And that may mean more than changing your makeup. They might ask you to make permanent changes. Such was the case with one of the world's most famous super-models.

When she first broke onto the modeling scene in the 1980s, Cindy Crawford was encouraged to remove her now-famous mole. The mod-eling industry did not like it and wanted it gone. They felt it was distracting—and no other top models had facial moles. Cindy was being asked to conform to a certain standard. Since she was just start-ing out—undoubtedly with big dreams and ambitions—she could have been swayed. We all know people who are willing to take drastic measures to please others. But Cindy said no. How cool is that? Cindy stood her ground. She risked her modeling career. But she did not want to change how she was made. And now her mole is one of her most defining physical attributes. She is perhaps even more popular and successful *because* of her mole—it is her own signature look. Bravo to her for not giving in to pressure!

What would you do if faced with the same situation? What is your defining physical attribute? If it were possible, would you ever change it? You may think it a thorn in your side, but to someone else, it just might be a rose.

Why is this important? Because God created *you* to be *you*! Only you can do what God made *you* to do. Think about it. No one else can be you. I think that's what Ephesians 1:11 means when it says, "It's in Christ that we find out who we are and what we are living for" (MSG). That gives me the confidence to focus on being the best me that I can be. That's the only thing in my control. It is pointless to compare myself to other women, especially in the entertainment world. I will always find someone skinnier or more beautiful than me. But I try to remember there is only one *me*. And there is only one *you*! Being different and unique is what's beautiful.

I am greatly encouraged by things like the Dove Real Beauty advertising campaign that shows regular women of all shapes and sizes. Calvin Klein frequently uses a plus-size model in their campaign. I love this because every single one of us needs to see that uniqueness is beautiful. Instead of telling women to conform to a certain size or shape, these campaigns encourage women to embrace their individuality and uniqueness.

After all, as supermodel Kathy Ireland says, "Beauty comes in all ages, colors, shapes, and forms. God never makes junk."

Some Days Are Better than Others

But what do you do when you simply have one of those bad days when you find yourself comparing yourself to other women? We all have bad days. I sure do. Sometimes I look in the mirror and wish I were different, or I look around and I wish I had her nose/mouth/hair/etc. Maybe you think you are too short, or too tall, or too thin, or too heavy. In high school I wished I had a smaller chest and longer hair. Even supermodels seem preoccupied with the one slight imperfection nobody else even notices. It seems that most of us women, to varying degrees, are not happy with the way God made us.

I have several dear friends who are both believers and professional models in New York City. I asked them how they deal with the business. My friend Christina, a successful model who has been on the cover of countless major magazines, shared this:

> As a model on set, the aim is to create an image or story. Sometimes that means a wholesome family on a holiday with my pretend children, husband, and parents, or a severe close-up of my face for beauty products, or walking down the runway in a beautiful but heavy ball gown while balancing in high heels. Although it can be amazing and fun, there are also times when I feel treated like an object: I am highly praised for my looks, or I have been handed clothing to wear that is transparent or been told to kiss and press closely against a male model I do not know . . . without any regard for my comfort level or personal convictions. These uncomfortable moments often require choices that need to be made on the spot, in front of the entire crew, and in a rushed atmosphere.
>
> Through experience, I have learned to be sure of my boundaries in advance, to ask a lot of questions about the job beforehand, and to look up the client in advance to see their brand and style. I have also made these boundaries clear to my agents so that I can try to avoid certain types of castings or bookings that I do not feel are in accordance with my standards. Sometimes it works out, and sometimes I show up and still need to make a decision. I desire to reflect the light of Christ in all I do, whether at work or in private. At the end of the day, this is a job, and this job is a chance for me to love people by how I conduct myself. I have learned that others' praise does not define who I am, or my value. That comes from God.

Remembering Where Your Value Comes From

But if not handled in a healthy way, body image can be taken to the extreme, and I certainly can relate to any girl who feels pressure in today's world to look a certain way. My friend Christina shared how she felt like an object and pressured to stay a certain size or look. The day after a major awards shows, like the Grammys or Oscars, *Inside Edition* will ask me to model dresses similar to the looks celebrities wore on the carpet. If you watch the red carpet coverage before those awards shows, you see how much attention the actresses get for their clothes. Well, often those sample replica dresses come in size 0 or 2—and neither of those is my size. So I have to ask for a larger size, and I have learned to alert the stylist to this.

Now, I would be lying if I said I didn't feel a twinge of shame or inferiority because of this. Then I remind myself I am doing my best. As I've said, I hit the gym and try to watch what I eat, but I'm just naturally a curvy girl. I will never be a size 2. That is not the body God gave me.

True love and acceptance do not come from changing ourselves. Psalm 139—I can't repeat this too often! I want you to get this!—states that God loves us just the way we are. The psalmist wrote, "I praise you because I am fearfully and wonderfully made; your works are wonderful, I know that full well (NIV)." *You* are already wonderful and I am already wonderful because God made us that way. That should be all that matters at the end of the day. We can strive to be the best we can be, but we should never forget that God loves us already . . . exactly as we are.

Just as He proclaimed His creation "good" in Genesis 1, He proclaims that we were made perfect in His sight. If we try too hard to change ourselves or focus too much on the physical, we are, in fact, disagreeing with how God made us.

When you look in the mirror, look confidently at your reflection. And don't be ashamed or frustrated with what you see, for you were made in the image of God, and He declares that you are fearfully and wonderfully made. My dear friend Teresa Swanstrom Anderson, blogger and author, shared this with me. She is the mother of six children, and two are girls. This is what she tries to share with her girls about true beauty. "I strive to teach my little ones that taking care of themselves is bringing glory to God. We need to care for what He has given us, which means taking care of our appearance in addition to our hearts. But we must continually keep examining our hearts and making sure our eyes are not drawn to the mirror for long, but focused on Him."

A Real-Life Vanity Test

A few weeks ago I realized, in practical terms, just how important my face is to my job.

I woke up one morning with my eyes puffy and swollen, and I had a slight red rash on my cheeks. I headed to the med clinic, and it was diagnosed as eczema. I was given several different medications, told by the doctor to keep my skin dry and clean, and to head home. But I had a story waiting for me to cover that day. What did I do? Well, I took those medications but promptly headed to work, put on my regular makeup, including my thick foundation for TV, and dashed to a presidential candidate's press conference in New York City. I filed a report that day for *Inside Edition*—rash and all. My makeup hid it pretty well, but I was still very self-conscious.

This experience reinforced that taking good care of my skin is essential to my job. If viewers saw the rash, they might focus on that and not hear the news story we had worked hard to put together. But guess who else is depending on my skin, in a sense? My producer, my photographer, my editor, my boss, and everyone who works on the show. They are expecting me to show up and do my job with little distraction. So I went to work the day of the diagnosis because I did not want to let anyone down. Some people might make a different decision, but I work in an industry where, literally, the show must go on.

Thankfully, my skin cleared up. I am not sure how I got the eczema in the first place. Could be stress, could be allergies, could be a reaction to my makeup. I ended up throwing away all my makeup and starting fresh, just to be sure. My face is part of my "uniform" at work, and I need to take care of that uniform to the best of my ability. That's just the reality of the business I'm in.

On a Practical Note . . .

Whenever I get a facial at a nice spa, I ask the aesthetician for her recommendations on skin-care products. As expected, she will usually recommend some super-expensive high-end line. I will listen politely and then say, "Thank you. That's a bit pricey for me right now. Could you recommend something less expensive, but still a good product?" The aesthetician almost always understands and gives me a second option. That's how I heard about the Korres line and Dermalogica products. (Dermalogica products work well for me. They are midrange in cost and soothing to my skin). Both Korres and Dermalogica are affordable and work really well. (You can find the Korres line at Sephora and Dermalogica at Ulta and most department stores.)

Takeaway

Living in our sexualized, image-obsessed culture can be hard, but it doesn't mean we have to hide and just hope for things to change. God made each and every one of us uniquely beautiful. So, for His glory, let's display that beauty for the entire world to see.

1. Remember that you are fearfully and wonderfully made. Just as parents root for their children to become the best they can be, God wants that from us for our good. He wants the world to see just how incredible He is through us as His children.

2. Find your style, one that is consistent with your faith and values.

3. Don't compromise your values to fit in with the world's definition and standards of beauty.

4. Take good care of yourself, for your "body is a temple of the Holy Spirit" (1 Corinthians 6:19).

*N*ew York is not an easy place to live and work. There is very good reason why Frank Sinatra sang, "If I can make it there, I'll make it anywhere." But Mr. Sinatra failed to mention that we need help if we actually are going to make it.

By the grace of God, when I was in New York City, I reconnected with a high school classmate who had the brilliant idea to start a women's Bible study at her apartment, and it was there I first met Megan. None of us knew it at the time, but we were all in for significant life changes. Some were wonderful changes like marriage, children, and, in my case, working on a new prime-time television show. Other changes were more difficult.

God never promised us that life would be easy, but through the hard times I have learned the importance of having friends you can lean on and—perhaps even more important—the gift of fellowship with women who will pray for you when you don't have any words left. I simply would not make it through the hard times without women who are seeking after God's heart . . . and are willing to share a little piece of their own hearts with me.

—Kelly Maguire, Fox News producer

Fourteen

The Modern-Day Proverbs 31 Woman

The Right Tools of Flexibility, Planning, and Organization

She is clothed in strength and dignity.
She can laugh at the days to come.

—PROVERBS 31:25 NIV

*Y*OU CAN DO IT ALL!

I cannot tell you how many female college students and twentysomethings have asked me, "How do you do it? I want to have a career like yours, but I also want kids. How can I have both? Won't I need to stay home with the kids?"

I can tell they are genuinely concerned—and I don't blame them! Both careers and families are highly demanding. It doesn't seem possible to manage both of them well and still have time to breathe. But I offer this truth to them and to you: you can have it all—thriving career, happy family, and personal satisfaction—but you can't have it all *perfectly*. You'll need to use multitasking tools, be organized, develop strong teamwork with your spouse, practice patience, prepare, and balance it all with biblical encouragement and guidelines. But it is absolutely possible.

I am passionate about sharing this message with millennial women because few people in the church seem to encourage this lifestyle. In fact, I think this is an issue that Christians have long danced around. And even if they encourage women to pursue their passions, there is no real handbook for how to do that. I hope this chapter will provide a blueprint for being a working woman and a wife and mother all at the same time.

I call this living up to your full potential! I also call it "channeling our inner Maya Angelou," because I love how she proclaimed *"I'm a woman phenomenally. Phenomenal woman, that's me."* Okay, phenomenal women, here we go. . . .

Choose Your Partner Carefully

If you think you desire the career-with-family lifestyle, choosing the right partner will be the most important decision you will ever make. Period.

So how do you make that choice? By using God's wisdom and your natural intelligence and by being honest from the start. My husband, Brian, knew when we first started dating just how ambitious I was. He knew all my dreams. We told each other everything. He knew I had huge hopes for my career and that I also wanted to have a family. So we started talking about what our life would look like if it accommodated his dreams and mine.

You might be reading this and thinking, *Oh, but if I'm that honest, I'll scare him away* or *What if I don't know yet what career I want to pursue?* Take heart. These are good things to reflect on right now. You are asking questions that so many of us ladies have asked before. But if you worry that you might frighten away your man, you may want to ponder this option: Is he the right man for you in the first place? Your future husband should be your biggest cheerleader!

And as for what career you want to pursue, right now is a great time to start taking some risks at work, and *then* consider marriage. I worked on my career and dated my husband until I was twenty-eight. He wanted to get married earlier; I did not. He respected my decision and knew establishing my career was very important to me. We both feel the timing ended up being the best choice for both of us. But we kept talking about that marriage date when we were dating!

If, after discussing your desires, your guy ends up intimidated, un-supportive, or even angry, he is probably not the right partner for you. We should never apologize for being honest and communicating openly. That is so important in a marriage and in life.

Plan to Be Flexible

A career in television has required me to be very adaptable and to relocate—often. I also work nights, holidays, and weekends. When I landed my first job, I knew that's what I was getting into. And in order for me to work nights and weekends, we knew Brian would need a more flexible job. Fortunately, Brian runs his own company and works as an event planner, so he is able to travel anywhere and work from there. His flexibility has been vital to my success.

This husband-wife and, later, parenting partnership will look dif-ferent for every person. For some of you, it will be mean that one of you works nights while the other works the day shift. One person might figure out a way to work from home in order for the other one to travel. The point is, you'll need to work out these details before, during, and sometimes even after the start of your career.

In practical terms, my job means that Brian and I have had to move according to my positions and assignments. So whenever my next job comes along, he has to pack up and change cities with me—and this is not easy! It means making new friends, finding a new church, and exploring new surroundings every time. But it also means Brian gets to see different parts of the country with me, which we have really come to value. And he meets some incredibly interesting people when he attends industry events with me. He's able to network in ways he couldn't if his job weren't flexible.

While this scenario may sound idyllic, it is not perfect. Plenty of times we miss our old friends, and we get tired of changing churches. We constantly talk about when and where we'll finally put down roots and what will work best for our family. We think we have found the perfect situation for us in Nashville, but we know my industry is ever changing and the job opportunities are unpredictable. When I moved to part-time work with *Inside Edition*, we did make the move to buy a house in Nashville, and now I commute every week to New York City for a few days. It's not easy, but we understand that sacrifice and un-orthodox solutions work best for our ambitious family.

The point is, you and your husband will need to keep talking and keep working to discover what will work best for the two of you as a couple and for your family before, during, and even after you start your career.

Discuss What Child Care Will Look Like

We knew that once we had children, child care would be an important issue to address. Some couples with young children are blessed to have grandparents who live nearby and can help. At first, we did not. When we had our first son, Chace, we lived in New York City, but all the grandparents lived in Seattle. For us, day care was an absolute necessity. We all know that child care is expensive, so it's another thing the two of you must discuss.

Will you hire a nanny or use a day-care facility? Will you be okay with leaving your child with other people? How many hours a week will your child stay in day care or be cared for by a nanny? When we had just one child, Brian and I decided we would take turns picking him up, and we would arrange our schedules to spend the maximum amount of time with him. For example, if I had an early assignment at work, Brian would stay home a little that morning with Chace; then I would leave work earlier that day and pick up Chace.

Regardless of the child care we arranged for the day, we knew we also needed to find good babysitters we trusted for emergencies. A friend gave me some great advice: find skilled babysitters before you need them. Get two or three numbers in your phone so that when you have a work conflict or something comes up, you already know people to call.

How do you find the best ones? I asked around for referrals and looked up child-care services in New York and in Nashville. And since my parents have since moved to the South, we also utilize their help.

To practice some of that organizing I mentioned earlier, I recommend this general approach to getting a handle on what your year will look like. On holidays, when the family is gathered, have everyone get out his or her calendar and plan for the coming year. (Plan to meet with your caregiver as well and then a few times throughout the year.) Mark on the calendar when each person has a big work event or a planned vacation. Then see how you can work together to support each other. Maybe one spouse will work from home one day a week so that both parents can maximize time with their kids. Or some people may choose to take the family along on work trips when possible. Here again, communication, planning, teamwork, and flexibility are key.

So, usually at Christmastime, Brian and I grab our calendars. I know ahead of time what big events I will be covering for *Inside Edition*. I have covered the last five Super Bowls, so I always mark off the last week of January and first week of February. I also write down the CMA Awards in November, the NFL draft in May, and my *Thursday*

Night Football games in the fall. Brian knows I will be traveling on those dates. Likewise, my husband's job calls for him to travel in the summer for his big conventions. We know June through August will be busy for him.

Once our big events are on the calendar, we see if he can work his schedule around my important dates and my schedule around his big commitments. When we can't, we plan for child care.

No two schedules will ever mesh perfectly, and Brian and I are constantly juggling. We are always glad we talked about our schedules early on. Better to be prepared than to be blindsided!

Teamwork and Organization

Growing up, I was not an orderly person. (Just ask my mom what my room looked like!) But with a busy career and bustling family life, I have learned to be organized. I realized I had to be if I wanted to succeed. College first taught me this. As I pursued my political science degree and each week faced tests, paper deadlines, presentations, student government, and a social life, I quickly saw that I would not survive without getting methodical. This will most likely be true for you, too, if you want to pursue a successful career and have a family.

You might be thinking, *Oh, this sounds like a quest for perfection!* Look at it this way: As author Christina Scalise says, "Organization isn't about perfection. It's about efficiency, reducing stress and clutter, saving time and money, and improving your overall quality of life."

Due to the breaking-news aspect of my industry, I quickly learned it is essential for me to stay organized on a personal level. I need to be ready to hop on an airplane anytime. So, in addition to having an updated passport and license, I need to keep my large purse stocked with items that would allow me to travel anywhere in the United States in a matter of hours. That's why I have my passport, license, insurance cards, credit cards, cash, phone, phone charger, makeup bag, and more in my purse at all times. And I added a cordless microphone this year—a habit I picked up early on at *Inside Edition*.

I was sitting at a café across the street from Central Park, having dinner with my husband, on the night Michael Jackson died. My phone rang in a matter of moments after the news broke. The *Inside Edition* office wanted to know how quickly I could be at the airport. I went from the café to the airport, never stopping at my apartment to pack clothes. But I had my purse, so I got on that plane, landed in LA that night, and figured out the rest later. This scenario has been repeated several times over the course of my seven years at the show, and every time I've been thankful my purse was well organized and well stocked with the essentials.

Think about what items you need for your work. If you want to be the best, it's not a bad idea to be ready at all times. As Abraham Lincoln said, "I will prepare and someday my chance will come." Be prepared and your chance will come!

Expect That Plans Fail Sometimes

If you plan to be a working mom, come to terms with these facts: you will be tired, you will miss out on some big moments and special events in your children's lives, and no one can do every single thing well all the time. For example, while I was very proud to cover the NFL in the fall of 2014, my son had just turned three years old and started flag football practice. I was covering a game in Denver on his first day of practice, so I had to watch via Facetime. It was not ideal, but I was thankful for technology that allowed me to at least watch him practice. Missing out is part of the reality of trying to do it all.

Brian and I have been fortunate to see the ideas I've mentioned work well for us. But despite our meticulous organization and careful planning, here's another fact: Mother Nature and the Lord will often change up everything!

I was thirty-six weeks pregnant with our second child when Brian left for a three-day work trip. It was his last trip before we both had planned to be home and await the baby's arrival. Everything had gone smoothly with our first baby—I had felt great, traveled to New York regularly, and was induced at 38.5 weeks—so I was expecting a repeat performance with baby number two.

But our second baby made his own decision! I felt contractions at midnight just as my husband landed in Seattle. I called him, told him I was on my way to the hospital, and said the baby was coming. He immediately got on another flight home, but he didn't make it in time. Our baby was born while he was flying somewhere over Kansas.

But here's where creativity can come in when things don't go perfectly. We had decided not to find out the gender. So while I was in the operating room getting my C-section, I announced to the staff that I did not want to find out the gender until my husband arrived. The staff thought I was crazy but obliged. Everyone referred to the baby as "it" until my husband walked into the room. Then we had a special moment together when we found out our baby was a boy.

Lesson here? You can plan and organize all you want, but God might have other designs for you. And be aware that Mother Nature can rearrange even the best-laid plans. When things don't go exactly as planned, improvise! (And if we have a third baby, I will ask my hubby not to travel after thirty-four weeks.)

Find What Works for You

Often when my husband and I attend dinner parties or church functions, people ask how we balance our careers and family life. Most people are quite amazed when they hear our story. They can't believe all the traveling I do and how supportive Brian is. We really are a team. People like to chime in and say, "We would kill each other! That would never work for us." Or "I don't know how you do it all. I certainly couldn't."

But we have learned to stop comparing ourselves to others. Brian and I have figured out what works for us, and that's all that matters. I fully realize our approach will not necessarily work for others, and their plans would probably not work for us! But, ladies, I am living my dream thanks to our family system. We are happy, our kids are happy, and we believe this is what God has called us to do. As long as God keeps opening doors for us, we will continue.

I encourage you to find the strategy that works for you, but don't compare your balancing act to other people's approaches. And don't be discouraged. Your talents, abilities, and situations are unique to you, but with some organization and planning, you can manage it all too.

If You Are Single . . .

What a wonderful time to be single! You have complete freedom to pursue your career and all your dreams. Take advantage of that!

I attended a small Christian college, and although it was pretty progressive, there was still a "ring by spring" attitude on campus. Lots of young women were keen on finding a husband before pursuing a career. There is nothing wrong with that choice. Marriage is a high calling. But if you feel as if you are called to do something else in life, you probably are. We are living in a time and a culture that support those dreams and desires. Pursue them wholeheartedly!

Opportunities for women exist as never before. We live in a nation that has had female Supreme Court justices, a female Speaker of the House, female candidates for president, and numerous strong females running businesses, such as Oprah Winfrey, Sheryl Sandberg, Meg Whitman, and Marissa Mayer. We see Megyn Kelly of Fox News and

Rachel Maddow of MSNBC as news anchors and Gail McGovern of the American Red Cross and model-turned-business-mogul Kathy Ireland as CEOs of nonprofits. This is a great time to go after your dreams. Pursue that master's degree, take an evening class on a subject you love, and enjoy the opportunities that come with living in this day and age.

Now, if you know already that you want to pursue your career and have a family, here are some practical thoughts I have gathered from both my experience and those of my single friends.

Get Out of Your Comfort Zone

Leave your comfort zone behind. In college, take a class on a subject unrelated to your major—just to broaden your horizons. And keep exploring for new interests after you graduate. I have loved acting and theater all my life. So when I moved to Nashville to pursue broadcasting, I quickly joined several things: a church, a gym where I could work out and meet people, and an acting class. The latter has proved to be one of the best decisions I ever made.

You see, most of us in the acting group will never make it in Hollywood, but we love the creative process and fun environment these classes provide. I have made numerous friends over the years in acting classes and, as a result, enjoy a really interesting and eclectic network of people. For you, instead of acting, it might be taking a music or yoga class or joining a softball team. Whatever it is, make time for it. This is a great way to meet people with similar interests.

When my friend Janelle was single and in her late twenties, she used to volunteer at church in all kinds of ministries that were out of her comfort zone, such as international mission meetings and microfinance meetings. She had initially thought God was calling her to Washington, DC, to work in politics. But she met some very interesting people at church, including her future husband, with whom she is now a missionary in Africa, implementing microfinance programs, and loving it. My friend Cindy decided to move from Seattle to Sun Valley, Idaho, after college because she loved skiing and wanted to live somewhere new. She met her future husband at a friend's party—one she almost didn't attend!

So try something new! Even if you don't meet your future spouse, you will meet exciting people, network, and likely walk away with a new friend or two.

Keep an Open Mind

Hollywood movies tell us that someday we will lock eyes with someone across the room, our hearts will beat superfast, he will ask us out on a romantic candlelit dinner, sparks will fly, and we will live happily ever after.

Not exactly.

I met my future husband at age twelve and I wasn't interested at all. I saw him off and on during summers in high school and college and knew some of his friends, but I assumed I would have more of the Hollywood moment when I met my future husband. But as I began pursuing my dreams, Brian became a friend who was incredibly supportive of my goals. He liked to hear me talk about my career ideas and family plans. He was also pursuing his own goals. We became really good friends in our twenties, and over time I realized he was a lot of what I had been dreaming of. I say this: don't count out those good friends. They can be really great partners, teammates, and spouses.

If You Have an Unhappy Relationship

If you are in a bad marriage, I encourage you to find a skilled, Bible-based marriage counselor. Despite being happily married seven years,

Brian and I are still in counseling. We have found it tremendously helpful through the rough patches that come because we are all human and life is tough. But one of the best statements I've ever heard about marital fighting: you've got too much to lose, especially if you have kids. Give your struggling relationship your best. Try to work it out.

My husband came from a broken home, and as a result he still struggles with some issues today. The world will tell you that all kids of divorce will be okay if the parents just love them enough. Well, yes and no, but by all means try to avoid divorce. Your kids have too much to lose. Find a good counselor who will help you with communication, healing, guidance—whatever's needed for you and your spouse.

If you are divorced and looking for a second chance at love, know that God is with you every step of the way. He can work out a Plan B!

One more thing: the benefits of being a working mom are huge. It's allowed me to live life to the fullest and tap into all that God has given me to do as a woman. I want this for every woman—especially you. So be strong and courageous!

Takeaway

1. Enjoying a successful career and full family life won't be easy, but it is possible!

2. It will require organization, hard work, communication, flexibility, and creativity.

3. Be brave as you pursue your faith, your family, and your career. It may seem scary and overwhelming at times, but God is always near. Look at what He told His servant Joshua:

"Be strong and courageous. Do not be afraid; do not be discouraged, for the LORD your God will be with you wherever you go" (Joshua 1:9 NIV).

4. If you decide to get married, who you pick as your partner is vital to your career goals.

*A*s an Olympic gymnast and a believer, I've encountered situations where I needed to stay true to who I was as a person and remember how I was raised. My mom taught me to believe in myself, work hard, and treat others with respect. In some situations I have had to make some tough decisions and deal with people saying really hurtful things. In the moment, I wanted to retaliate, but decided not to. I've found that it's always better to take the high road and stay true to my beliefs.

Three months before the 2012 Olympic Games, I seriously injured my ankle. Of course I was filled with a lot of questions and doubts, but at the same time I knew that my heavenly Father would never leave me or forsake me; I drew upon the scriptures I had meditated on my whole life. I learned that it's in the most challenging times that you have to rely on your faith the most and never give up!

In this book, Megan offers similar stories and examples of how a believer can succeed and flourish but never forget who they are.

—Gabby Douglas, Olympic gold medalist, gymnastics

Fifteen

Remember Who You Are

Stories from the Frontlines

It takes nothing to join the crowd.
It takes everything to stand alone.

—HANS F. HANSEN

*H*I, MEGAN, *I just sent you the script for this part. It's for a major television drama. Please put it on tape and get back to me ASAP. I think you have a great shot at getting this!"*

I listened to this voicemail from an acting agent I had just begun working with in New York. I checked my email and found the script. My lines were clearly highlighted and I only had a few. They wanted me to play a reporter just arriving to the scene of a crime. I read the lines again. It seemed simple enough. I glanced at the dialogue just before my scene. The script they sent me included the page for the prior scene leading up to mine. My heart sank as I read. It was a sex scene, and it was very graphic and explicit. In that context, I just couldn't do the part. This was not something I was comfortable putting my name on. I emailed my agent and told them I was sorry, but I would not be able to get them the taped lines in time. The agent immediately emailed back and asked me to reconsider. They added that this was a big show and I was one of only a few up for the role. Why couldn't I try to make this work? As I read the message I bit my lip. Saying no often runs you the risk of being cast to the bottom of the barrel of opportunities. In other words, if I said no to this part, there was a chance this agent would never call me again. But I was willing to take that risk. That type of role was not me. I emailed back and firmly said no. I never heard from that particular acting agent again. But as you have read in this book, this was not the end of my acting career. I eventually got another agent, and I have booked roles I am comfortable with. It's important to remember who you are.

✦   ✦   ✦

When you finally get the dream job, birth or adopt a baby, start the nonprofit, finish your college degree, or reach the level of success you've always dreamed about—when you finally get the seat at the table you've always wanted—beware. You could be in a pretty vulnerable place.

I have watched friends go to Los Angeles or New York in search of that special position, fame, or fortune and slowly lose their once strong and godly character. Friends who committed to staying pure until marriage eventually justified living with their significant others. Individuals who never swore or cursed let those foul words sneak into their daily vocabulary. And passionate believers who consistently attended church suddenly found it the easiest thing to eliminate when they got that promotion at work.

Oh, but these are the demands of the real world! you may be thinking. *These behaviors are unavoidable. You have to fit in. It's not a big deal.* Is it not?

DeVon Franklin, one of my heroes, is a top producer in Hollywood. He is someone who climbed the ladder but never lost his fierce dedication to his faith. He is the entertainment mogul famous for always observing the Sabbath—even while on a movie set. Every Sabbath, DeVon faithfully turns off his cell phone and email. Then, from sunrise to sunset, he seeks the Lord and engages only in spiritual activities. (To find out more about DeVon, read his fascinating book *Produced by Faith*.)

Likewise, NFL quarterback Tim Tebow and Super Bowl Seahawks champion Russell Wilson passionately express their Christian beliefs from their platforms as successful professional athletes. Both are outspoken about attending church, maintaining their conservative dating standards, and praising God in victory and in defeat. Tim Tebow gives glory to God in a very public display on the football field, kneeling and bowing his head at various victorious moments throughout the game. And Russell Wilson is vocal about his faith in God in interviews and on social media. This did not change when he won—or, the very next year, lost—the Super Bowl. These athletes demonstrate that it is possible to be faithful believers while experiencing amazing fame and success. These guys keep in mind who they are.

At My Office

Even if you're not as outspoken as Tim Tebow or don't have the platform of Russell Wilson, being confident in your faith is an important part of remembering who you are. People often ask if I have ever felt persecuted for my faith or been mocked in the newsroom for being a Christian. I can truthfully tell them and you, no, not once. My boss and colleagues are neutral on the issue of religion. They respect that I attend church; they simply don't choose to do so themselves. Therefore, religion and faith don't come up naturally in conversation. It's just not something on their minds. But I've never felt criticized for my beliefs.

Now, I am not the most outspoken person about my faith. I really believe that actions speak louder than words. And, as I stated before, when my coworkers ask how my weekend was, I speak up. I let them know I attended church because it's important to me, and though they genuinely look surprised, they never respond negatively. Usually they just nod or change the subject. But sometimes someone will ask a follow-up question or two. And that's when I have the opportunity to talk about my faith.

My boss respects that I am a Christian and that I attend church and Bible studies. He is also a businessman who is well aware of the surprising success of movies like *God's Not Dead* and the popularity of the History channel's *The Bible* miniseries. He recognizes that a large portion of the country is religious, and he occasionally comes to me for story ideas about the role of faith in the entertainment industry. In fact, because of my friendship with *The Bible* producers Roma Downey and Mark Burnett, who are believers, *Inside Edition* got several interviews with them during the series run.

Remembering who you are is not always easy in a business setting. I think Satan uses stress and enticing distractions to slowly pull us away from the Lord. In New York City, for instance, there are always exciting things to do, such as go to movie premieres, launch parties, cocktail mixers, outdoor concerts—you name it! And the energy of the city makes you feel as though you need to be doing something. It's very hard for me to relax in the Big Apple. This restlessness, though, has been great for my job because I am highly motivated to keep working, keep meeting people, and keep furthering my career. But I have to be careful because these things can start filling up my life.

And then I can suddenly find that I'm the one skipping the weekly Bible study I started, justifying it by saying I'll do it only this once and get back on track next week. Then I get an invitation to go to the Hamptons for a weekend and miss church again. Or I just choose to sleep in on Sunday morning because I am so exhausted from the workweek.

At first, we don't think these things will damage our spiritual lives. But I believe these little compromises are Satan's sneaky ways of slowly luring our focus away from God and getting us off track. I see it happen all the time in the lives of people who, like me, are very ambitious. That's why I have to continually remind myself that I am a Christian and my primary desire is to please God, not myself.

Salt and Light

When facing invitations that compromise our beliefs, what can we do to maintain our spiritual integrity and remember who we are?

Matthew 5:13–14 offers two great principles for Christians in any field. Jesus described His followers as "the salt of the earth" and "the light of the world" (NIV). And He points out that if salt loses its flavor, it is worthless. For me, being salt means reading my Bible regularly, staying engaged in Bible study with fellow believers, and maintaining a spirit of optimism, hope, and truth. For me, being light means avoiding such evil as gossip, slander, and cheating. It means staying positive by not complaining and working hard and following through on projects and assignments.

I think we are also light when we are the same person at work as we are at play. Have you ever met people who act differently based on where they are and whom they are with? They act or talk a certain way at work or school and then change their behavior when they are out with their friends. I think we are meant to be salt and light wherever we are.

So when we have a seat at the table, what can we do to be God's light and salt?

Friendly Reminders

I need regular reminders of what kind of person God wants me to be—and I have been giving these to myself for years. When I was in high school, I started putting little notes on my bathroom mirror, on my bedroom door, and in my locker at school. On these notes I wrote my favorite Bible verses, inspirational sayings, or the lyrics of worship songs. I took this habit with me to college, decorating my dorm room with these cards and putting them inside my car and my wallet. When I entered the workforce, I transferred this routine to my apartment, my desk, and my workspace. These little notes remind me, every day and several times a day, who I am.

Be Accountable to Someone

Another way to ensure that you are being God's salt and light is to have a strong group of Christian friends or accountability partners whom you see regularly. I have a circle of girlfriends in New York who desire to maintain their spiritual lives while building powerful careers. We get together for coffee or dinner and discuss how to keep our faith strong. You wouldn't believe how helpful this is. To stay faithful to God when we work in the public marketplace, we need people who help us stay on His path.

So wherever you are in your life or career, find several people you admire and ask them to hold you accountable. My Bible study friends in New York City send out emails each week reminding us to read our assigned chapters and put those Bible verses into action. We also remind each other to pray not only for our families but also for our workplaces. And when we feel discouraged about our jobs, we ask each other for support and remind each other that God is in control and that we should boldly seek His wisdom. One of our favorite verses is "Because of Christ and our faith in him, we can now come boldly and confidently into God's presence" (Ephesians 3:12 NLT). I cannot always remember these truths alone. Christian friends and the accountability they offer provide needed support for holy living. I encourage you to find your own accountability partners who will encourage you in your career and life.

Write a Personal Mission Statement

I took a wonderful leadership class in college in which we were asked to write a short, personal mission statement that explained who we were, what we believed in, and what we desired to do with our lives. Here's what I wrote as a college sophomore:

> *I, Megan Alexander, am a cherished child of God. I am a happy, optimistic, and smart person who loves working hard and setting goals. I will strive to reach my full potential in all aspects of my life. I will honor my family in all I do and strive to treat others as I want to be treated. I will represent Jesus in all areas of my life and keep having fun until He comes back!*

As I write this book, I am thirty-five years old. Have I lived out this personal mission statement every day? No. At times I totally forgot I had a mission statement! I certainly have not always felt happy, optimistic, or smart, and too often I definitely did not treat others as I wanted to be treated. But guess what? Looking at my mission statement every so often has helped keep me on track. And I have made some edits to it along the way as goals have been reached or circumstances have changed.

Posting note cards and writing a mission statement may seem like little things to do, but it's the little, everyday things that make a world of a difference when you are sitting in your office (at home or in another location), looking at the work piled high on your desk or countertop, and knowing you have a million decisions to make about your career, your personal life, your family, and your spiritual well-being.

What about you? Who are you? Who do you want to be? What habits do you want to maintain, and which ones would you like to lose? What goals do you have for your faith? What specific steps will help you reach them? Take some time to answer these questions and then consider developing your own personal mission statement. It doesn't need to be complicated. But think about who you want to be as God's child and set your standards high. Then tuck it away somewhere safe and pull it out every so often. Better yet, hang it in plain sight—on your bathroom mirror, at your desk at work, or in the car—as a friendly reminder so you can remember who you are.

Whether you're a mom, or you work from home, or you're in that corner office, remember your mission statement. If you want to stay on the path of righteousness, it can be a valuable tool. Without a mission statement that includes specific goals, we don't know where we're headed. Paul reminded us in Philippians 3:13–14 (NIV), "Forgetting what is behind, and straining toward what is ahead, I press on toward the goal to win the prize for which God has called me heavenward in Christ Jesus."

Making the Tough Call

At the beginning of this chapter, you read about an acting role I needed to pass on. Remembering who you are means making tough, sometimes unpopular decisions.

As I've mentioned, a few years ago Mark Burnett and Roma Downey produced *The Bible* miniseries for the History channel. I was a superfan of the show. Every week I invited my friends in NYC to my apartment to watch the series, and we would discuss it afterward. It was a special time in my life, and I will always cherish the memories. As such a fan, I was thrilled when *Inside Edition* covered the media events several times during the series run.

The first few weeks of the series covered the Old Testament, and the middle weeks covered the New Testament. During the New Testament weeks, when viewers were introduced to Satan's character for the first time, a certain headline appeared in several newspapers and websites. Someone decided that Satan looked a lot like President Barack Obama. Did the casting agents purposely choose an actor who looked like President Obama to play Satan? In my industry, a dramatic headline gets press, and this story stayed front-page news for a few days. My boss wanted me to ask Roma Downey and Mark Burnett about it, so I interviewed them while they were in New York. Roma and I had become friendly acquaintances, and she was aware that I had been watching the show every Sunday night.

Just as my photographer was setting up his camera and our interview was about to begin, Roma looked at me and quietly said something like "Please don't ask about Satan and Obama. We should be talking about Jesus. This [discussion of Satan and Obama] is a distraction from more important topics."

I was immediately faced with a dilemma. This topic was the sole reason I was interviewing Mark and Roma. My boss expected me to ask that very question. I took a deep breath and silently asked the Lord, *What should I do? It's my job, as a reporter, to ask questions.* But here I was, a Christian, being asked by a sister in Christ not to ask a certain question.

I happened to agree with Roma: Why was the media focusing on how the character of Satan allegedly looked like Obama instead of how Satan tempted Jesus and how we are tempted in our own lives? The Satan/Obama connection created a buzz, and that buzz generated more attention and ratings. But for Roma and me, it was frustrating that we were even talking about it. I decided not to ask Roma and Mark that question. And after the interview, Roma grabbed my hand, looked at me with tears in her eyes, and said, "Thank you. Thank you. You are a soul sister."

I believe I honored God that day when I redirected the questions; I think I was salt and light. But then I had to take that next step—and it wasn't easy! I had to tell my boss I did not ask the question. I explained Roma's request and added that my gut told me I should not. I told him I thought it was a deal-breaker, that if I asked that question, *Inside Edition* would never again get invited to Roma's press conferences. My boss was annoyed at first, but he came to understand and trust my judgment. He also knew the value of maintaining a strong relationship with Roma. He saw the potential for future interviews as well. (Remember, this is the man who is the master of advancing the story!)

I realize it was a risk to do this, and I had to carefully weigh all options and be honest with my boss. Listen, I was fortunate. I realize sometimes in business disobeying your supervisor can lead to dire consequences. Don't make a bold move without careful prayer and, when possible, wise counsel.

In this case, it ended up working out. Later, when Roma announced that she and Mark were remaking the legendary film *Ben-Hur*, I was one of the first she granted an interview.

Being salt and light is not easy, and it won't always end on a happy note or with an earthly reward. But honoring God is our purpose as believers, and something we should always strive to do.

You Want Me to Wear *That*?

Sometimes the situation won't be as dramatic as changing a nationally televised interview but will instead require quiet, personal conviction.

When *Inside Edition* covers awards shows, we report on the award winners and cover what some of the celebrities wear. In fact, sometimes who wore what is more important than who won what! A day or two after the Oscars or Grammys, we will choose the three or four most popular celebrity dresses. Then several models and I will wear them to show our viewers how they can get a similar look, for less money.

Well, at one particular event Kim Kardashian wore a white dress that was very low-cut and revealing. When I arrived at the shoot location in Manhattan, my producer informed me that I would be modeling a less-expensive version of Kim Kardashian's dress. My gut twisted. I looked at the white gown hanging up in my dressing room. Just like her dress, it would show lots of cleavage. I was concerned about wearing that dress, let alone modeling it on national television. I was raised to believe that my body is a temple of the Lord and I just wasn't comfortable showing that much skin—and I liked being covered up.

I told the stylist I wasn't comfortable with this particular dress and asked if I could switch to another gown. Usually, as long as I wear one of the three or four dresses, it is fine. But this particular day the stylist was adamant that I wear the Kardashian dress. She said all the other models had been assigned their dresses and were starting hair and makeup based on those looks. In other words, the wheels were in motion, and I was threatening to slow down the process.

These shoots are very stressful, and one reason is that time is usually tight. I knew the stylist didn't want to switch up the dresses and models because it would take time. But I pushed back. I politely asked to see the other dresses. Heidi Klum had worn a short black dress, and we happened to have a similar option that was cute, fairly conservative, and much more my style. I took it back to the stylist and said, "Please let me wear this dress. This black dress is much more my style, and I need to feel good about this shoot. My boss will notice if I lack confidence when I wear this dress." (I realized this last part at the last minute. It's true! If I'm not authoritative on air, I reflect poorly on my show.)

The stylist begrudgingly let me switch dresses, another model ended up wearing the Kardashian dress, and the shoot went just fine. I felt good because I had stuck to my convictions and maintained my standards even when people fought me. I honored God with my modesty. I remained polite but firm. I also offered a Plan B—the Heidi Klum dress. This may seem like a small battle, but it was important to me. I wanted my actions to be salt and light on that set.

Again, being salt and light is not easy; it may require you to stand up when you're not comfortable doing so. It's much easier to know who you are and make that decision, rather than having to decide who you are in that moment. Aristotle said "Knowing thyself is the beginning of wisdom." Knowing your goals, your boundaries, your risk level—having these figured out beforehand—will save you time, potential stress, and heartache, and equip you with a strong sense of your faith and self that is invaluable in the competitive and fast-paced workplace and in life.

Takeaway

1. Know who you are. Write a mission statement. You'll have a better chance keeping your saltiness if you define who you are in the first place.

2. Stay accountable to someone: find some friends who will remind you who you are.

3. When you face a situation that will change who you are, ask God to provide you with wisdom and strength to work out the problem in a way that maintains your values and standards.

I've had the unexpected role of working with actors, athletes, leaders in the media, business and government officials, and everyday people who found themselves having to live out their faith in the spotlight. All of these people share the struggle of staying true to their Christian values in the face of enormous pressure. I'm so thankful that Megan has written this book to shine a light on the fact that it is indeed possible to stay faithful to God in a culture that is, for the most part, at odds with that faith. As my longtime friend Darrell Green, who played twenty seasons for the Washington Redskins and is in the NFL Hall of Fame, repeatedly tells me, "Keeping close to people of faith kept me close to Christ."

It's easy to impress those who only know you from a distance. We believers must stay humble and recognize both our daily need for God's strength and the fact that it comes through the encouragement of people who really know us. Being faithful to a few simple life principles will mean the difference between success or failure in this all-important drama of living out your faith in the public eye.

There is no greater joy.

—Dr. Rice Broocks, cofounder of Every Nation Ministries, author of *God's Not Dead* and *Man, Myth, Messiah*

Sixteen

The Finals Are Never Over

Once You Are There, Stay Strong

For what does it profit a man
to gain the whole world, and forfeit his soul?

—MARK 8:36

*I*T IS MY SINCERE HOPE that as you've read these pages, you have not only been inspired and encouraged to pursue your dreams and goals, but you have also been given some practical tools to get there. My experience is obviously in the media world, but the stories and principles in this book can be applied to any career. At the end of the day, success in a chosen career requires such basics as hard work, persistence, a positive attitude, knowing yourself and your faith, and making the best decisions in accordance with your values. I also hope this book helped you believe you really can live out your faith in a difficult industry and still be successful.

We hear a lot about the entertainment industry having no soul. Often when I hear this, I think of Mark 8:36, quoted above. If we have a soul, how do we work in this industry? As this book showed through stories and examples, we do it step by step: keeping our faith in Jesus, and living in a way that honors Him. It is an ongoing process. The journey will never be over, and every day we start again. Every day we will face a new situation at work, in our family, or in life. C. S. Lewis stated, "Relying on God has to begin all over again every day as if nothing had yet been done." As my father said to me when I graduated college, "Meg, the finals are never over."

You may find yourself in the corner office one day, or sitting in that boardroom, or anchoring that national newscast, or auditioning for that big part. And at one point you might look around and say, "Wow, I made it! I got here!"

But in a sense, we will never "make it" in this world. Because our prize is something greater than anything the world offers. It will be that moment we arrive at the Pearly Gates. And our Father, the Creator of this world and the Maker of all things, will either say to us, "I never knew you, depart from Me," or "Well done, good and faithful servant" (Matthew 7:23 NASB and 25:21 NIV).

Which will He say to you? What will He say about your contribution to this world? I try to think about this every single day.

Audience of One

When the pressure gets to be too much or I feel pulled in too many directions, or I'm overwhelmed with this daunting task of actually putting my faith into action in this large and powerful industry, I take a deep breath and try to remember that, in the end, I am performing for an audience of one.

One of my favorite things to do before a big event is play Toby-Mac's song "Lose My Soul." It beautifully summarizes the ongoing struggle believers will face in this world until we get to the next— struggles that will chip away at our integrity and tempt us to make decisions that are counter to our faith. He equates the struggle to that of being a child at a three-ring circus and wanting to run into each ring to join in all the excitement. And the only way not to lose our souls is to keep our eyes fixed on the ultimate goal, and try to remember whom we are performing for.

Go for It!

As you step into the spotlight in life and in your career, keep your eyes on Jesus. And when you fall short, remember the good news: we serve a God who loves us and wants us to succeed. So get back up and keep on going! You *can* thrive in your career while staying true to your beliefs. Now *go for it!* I'm cheering you on!

—Megan

Acknowledgments

TO MY SONS, Chace and Catcher—may you pursue the dreams and desires of your heart, and as you do so, hold your family, friends, and faith close. It is a gift to be your mom.

To my parents for challenging me to be more than I ever thought I could be. You raised up a child in the way she should go (Proverbs 22:6 NIV). I am forever grateful for the time, energy, and love you have poured into me.

To the rockstar team behind my book: My amazing editor, Lisa Stilwell—thank you for your talent and patience, and for answering my numerous emails! Also Jennifer Smith, Rob Birkhead, Ami McConnell, Jonathan Merkh, and everyone at Simon & Schuster and Howard Books—thank you for believing in this project!

To Wes Yoder, Becky Nesbitt, and Julia Bonner for your feedback and hard work on my behalf.

To all my incredible book contributors—for sharing your hearts and wisdom.

To my *Inside Edition* family—for teaching me how to share stories with the world. Thank you, Charles Lachman, for the support and encouragement.

To my incredible partner in life, my husband, Brian. Thank you for being my biggest fan, loudest cheerleader, and teammate in life. So much of this book is because of our partnership. God gave me the greatest gift when he brought you into my life. I love dreaming big with you!

And finally, to all the teachers, coaches, bosses, and friends who ever shared a kind word or thought with me—those words matter and they are remembered. It's my honor to now Pay It Forward.

About the Author

*M*EGAN ALEXANDER is a national news correspondent with CBS television and can be seen every evening as a correspondent on the longest-running, top-rated syndicated national newsmagazine television show *Inside Edition*. She is also a special correspondent for CBS television with the team at *Thursday Night Football*, covering the games and related stories for all CBS affiliates around the world. Megan has covered the last six Super Bowls, major awards shows, and national political events. She serves as a guest commentator on the *Wendy Williams Show* and *Showbiz Tonight* on HLN.

Previously she has worked for KENS 5 in San Antonio, Texas; Fox 17 in Nashville, Tennessee; and KEYT in Santa Barbara, California. She got her start in radio at Metro Networks. She has also hosted the popular FUEL youth devotional series for LifeWay. She graduated from Westmont College with a degree in Political Science and International Relations. She grew up in Seattle, Washington, and attended King's Schools.

Megan regularly speaks to groups and conferences. She was the keynote speaker for the Powerful Women Paving the Way conference at Penn State Business College. She sits on the board of the Hugh O'Brian Youth Leadership organization (HOBY) and is an executive producer and actor in the feature film *Heartbeats*.

Megan splits her time between New York City and Nashville, Tennessee. She and her husband are the proud parents of two sons. She also adores her dog Indiana, eating chocolate, sleeping in, and singing karaoke.

For more on Megan, go to www.MeganAlexander.com and connect with her on Facebook, Twitter, and Instagram.